W9-BVV-838

Aging in Place:
The Role of Housing
and Social Supports

ABOUT THE EDITOR

Leon A. Pastalan, PhD, is Professor of Architecture in the College of Architecture and urban Planning at the University of Michigan. Dr. Pastalan is also Director of the National Center on Housing and Living Arrangements for Older Americans. As a researcher of long standing in the field of environments for the elderly, he is an expert in sensory deficits, spatial behavior, and housing. Dr. Pastalan has published many books and articles resulting from his work, including *Man Environment Reference 2 (MER 2),* (The University of Michigan Press, 1983), *Retirement Communities: An American Original* (The Haworth Press, 1984), and most recently, *Lifestyles and Housing of Older Adults: The Florida Experience* (The Haworth Press, 1989). Dr. Pastalan is also the editor of the *Journal of Housing for the Elderly* (The Haworth Press).

Aging in Place:
The Role of Housing
and Social Supports

Leon A. Pastalan
Editor

The Haworth Press
New York • London

Aging in place

Aging in Place: The Role of Housing and Social Supports has also been published as *Journal of Housing for the Elderly*, Volume 6, Numbers 1/2 1990.

The Haworth Press, Inc., 10 Alice Street, Binghamton, NY 13904-1580
EUROSPAN/Haworth, 3 Henrietta Street, London WC2E 8LU England

Library of Congress Cataloging-in-Publication Data

Aging in place : the role of housing and social supports / Leon A. Pastalan, editor.
    p. cm.
    "Has also been published as Journal of housing for the elderly, volume 6, numbers 1/2 1990" – T.p. verso.
    Includes bibliographical references.
    ISBN 0-86656-981-2 :
    1. Aged – Housing – United States. 2. Aged – Services for – United States. I. Pastalan, Leon A., 1930- .
HD7287.92.U54A38   1990
363.5'946'0973 – dc20

90-34022
CIP

$29.95
BK

Aging in Place: The Role of Housing and Social Supports

CONTENTS

Preface   ix
  Leon A. Pastalan

Chapter 1: Supportive Relationships in Shared Housing   1
  Jon Pynoos
  Lisa Hamburger
  Arlyne June

  Data and Methodology   3
  Survey Results   4
  Discussion   19
  Conclusion   23

**Chapter 2: Supporting the Independence of Elderly
  Residents Through Control Over Their Environment**   25
    Ellen Feingold
    Elaine Werby

  Introduction   25
  Organization   26
  Enhancing Control   27
  Case Study   29
  Costs and Conflicts   30
  Conclusion   32

**Chapter 3: Living Arrangements and Informal Social
  Support Among the Elderly**   33
    Andrew Wister

  Methodology   35
  Results   37
  Discussion   40

Chapter 4: The Housing and Support Costs of Elderly with Comparable Support Needs Living in Long-Term Care and Congregate Housing   **45**
Leonard F. Heumann

Introduction   45
Previous Cost Comparison Research   47
Cost Comparison in the Middle West   52
Conclusions   69

Chapter 5: A Comparison of the Functional Status of Older Adults Living in Congregate and Independent Housing   **73**
Veronica F. Engle

Method   74
Results   77
Discussion   79

Chapter 6: Which Elderly Home Owners Are Interested in Accessory Apartment Conversion and Home-Sharing   **87**
David P. Varady

Introduction   87
Methods   90
Findings   93
Conclusions and Policy Implications   97

Chapter 7: Senior Resident vs. Senior Highrise — Liability for Transferring Elderly Residents   **101**
Leonard H. Hellman

Chapter 8: Influence of Income on Energy Beliefs and Behaviors of Urban Elderly   **107**
Colleen K. Mileham
Jeanette A. Brandt

Background   108
Methodology   110
Findings   114
Implications   120

**Chapter 9: Continuing/Life Care Facilities and
the Continuum of Care**   **125**
        Diane E. Alperin
        Nicholas D. Richie

Introduction   125
Procedure   126
Findings   127
Discussion   128
Conclusion   129

Preface

In this special issue a number of crucial factors will be discussed regarding the role of social supports and the impact it has on a person's independence, specifically as it relates to living arrangements. One of the important goals for housing that has emerged in the past few years has been aging in place. Aging in place means many things to many people but for our purposes it means not having to move from one's present residence in order to secure necessary support services in response to changing needs. The changes that most frequently precipitate a residential relocation are health, death of spouse or loss of income.

The variety of living arrangements are very extensive and it would be instructive to remind ourselves of how our elders live. We know, for instance, that more than two-thirds of older non-institutionalized persons live in a family setting. We also know that while approximately 80% of the men live in family settings only slightly over half of all older women do. It's also important to point out that the proportion living in a family setting decreased with age, so that the older the person, the more likely he or she will be living alone or with non-relatives.

It should also be pointed out that of the 19 million households headed by older persons in 1987, fully three-quarters were home owners and one-quarter were renters. This housing is generally older and less adequate than the balance of the nation's housing with almost half of these units being built before 1950. The percentage of income spent on housing (excluding maintenance and repairs) was 17% for home owners and 35% for renters.

Faced with declining physical capabilities and incomes as well as loss of spouse many older adults are confronted with constraints which severely restrict aging in place opportunities. For these vulnerable individuals, housing needs cannot be met simply by providing shelter alone. By effective use of social services, access to a variety of housing choices can be opened up. Home health care, home-delivered meals, maintenance and repairs, energy and weatherization programs, homemaker chore services, and accessibility to transportation can enable many elderly households to remain in their homes, and may also expand the types of housing alternatives available to individuals who would otherwise be restricted in their options because of changes in marital status and declining health and income.

Presently there are many serious gaps in the provision and in the coverage of housing-related services. Much of the current services policy has relied heavily on nursing homes to meet the needs of those older adults who require some assistance in performing daily tasks. Few support mechanisms have existed which help older Americans cope with changes in their health, economic, and social environments. Other gaps in coverage include: (1) an inadequate overall preventive policy for keeping individuals out of institutions; (2) very few services targeted to the needs of homeowners; (3) what services are available are spread out under a variety of programs; (4) a lack of information regarding services which are available; and (5) residents of rural areas have typically been without assistance due to the lack of mechanisms for the provision of services. Consequently, programs are duplicated in some areas, and lacking in others.

In summary there are increasing numbers of older Americans who are faced with sharp and drastic cuts in disposable income upon retirement and changes in marital and health status all of which tends to make remaining in their residence increasingly more difficult. Without the necessary supports many may have no other choice but to be prematurely or inappropriately placed in costly health care facilities or be forced to move into unfamiliar, less safe, and less desirable housing environments and neighborhoods.

The authors in this publication explore some of the dimensions associated with aging in place. Pynoos, for example, presents some strong evidence that supportive relationships are very important in a shared housing arrangement in terms of fellow residents providing frail persons with significant amounts of assistance and thereby helping to keep persons in familiar surroundings.

Feingold feels that increasing loss of control over one's life is associated with reduced independence among the elderly. She discusses how competence is enhanced by providing residents with genuine control over their lives and through access to real choices in necessities in social contacts, in services and facilities.

Wister deals with the increasing phenomenon of North Americans living alone. He describes how elders who choose to live alone appear to sacrifice some degree of mutual exchange for privacy and independence. How they also tend to rely on friendship to a greater extent than those who reside with others. Implications for support services and changes in the family are discussed in the context of living arrangement selection in later life.

Heumann deals with congregate housing as an alternative to nursing care for those elderly too frail for less supportive housing. The author presents a thesis based on different assumptions about age and capital cost, reimbursement methods and level of resident functional ability that significant savings can be attributed to congregate housing.

Engle reports that functional status of congregate housing residents did not differ from older adults living in independent housing as measured by the Sickness Impact Profile. In terms of independence, however, congregate residents tended to use supportive services to maintain their level of independence rather than to attain independence.

Varady found in his study that in order to stay in place a number of resident, particularly those who were under financial stress, had a high interest in accessory apartment conversion and/or home-sharing. These findings were based on the response of middle class suburban home owners which suggest the wide appeal of such programs regardless of socio-economic status or residential location.

Hellman raises a most pertinent point regarding the basic lack of a clear discharge policy for most senior housing situations. He maintains that such a lack opens housing providers to be sued for liability. The author goes on to develop an objective basis for a well grounded discharge policy.

Although public attention toward residential energy costs has diminished, belief in the seriousness of the energy problem remains a concern for the elderly according to Mileham and Brandt. Their research indicates that urban elderly with lower incomes engage in significant lifestyle cutbacks and are adversely affected by energy costs. Policies and programs should address the needs of this type of elderly person particulary as it may impact on aging in place.

Finally Alperin and Richie reveal in their study of continuing care/life care facilities that many of these alleged full service communities do not actually have a full range of services. For example, when a person needs home health services only slightly more than half of the facilities in the sample had such services available. The study calls into question the extent to which such facilities actually provide services at discrete points on the proposed continuum of care, rather than mainly at the two extreme locations, the resident's apartment or the skilled nursing home.

Leon A. Pastalan, PhD
Editor

Chapter 1

Supportive Relationships in Shared Housing

Jon Pynoos
Lisa Hamburger
Arlyne June

SUMMARY. This study surveyed a random sample of 144 house sharers of one of the country's oldest matching programs to investigate which types of persons house share, reasons that people choose house sharing, the types of assistance house sharers need and provide for each other and the types of housing sharing relationships that exist. It found that primary reasons for sharing were financial (44%), companionship (21%), and help in home and health care (19%). Almost one-third of housesharers were frail and while they received a significant amount of assistance from their partners in household tasks, not all of them were in matches in which services were provided or exchanged. And, contrary to other research that suggests matches are not conducive to intimacy, almost half the sample indicated moderate to strong levels of friendship as well as willingness to confide in their partners on personal matters.

The availability of affordable and supportive housing is an increasing concern for frail older persons. Solutions such as public

Jon Pynoos, PhD, is Associate Professor of Gerontology and Urban Planning and Director, Program in Policy and Services Research, Andrus Gerontology Center, University of Southern California, University Park, MC 0191, Los Angeles, CA 90089-0191.

Lisa Hamburger, BS, is Research Assistant, Dual Masters Degree Candidate in Urban Planning and Gerontology, University of Southern California.

Arlyne June, MA, is Executive Director, Project Match, 1671 Park Avenue, San Jose, CA 95126.

Appreciation is extended to Jim Corcoran who conducted the telephone interviews and Mary Jackson who assisted in the data analysis.

1

housing have been curtailed and programs such as congregate housing have never gone beyond the demonstration phase. The federal government is now promoting community-based alternatives intended to make better use of existing resources. In response, a spectrum of services and support system networks has been developed to enhance the present housing environment of the elderly and, as a consequence, improve their well-being. One such system is shared housing.

Shared housing programs attempt to match residents, known as *providers*, who have extra living space in their apartment or home with unrelated individuals, known as *seekers*, including couples or single parents with children. In contrast to most senior citizen services which are delivered to the home or provided at community focal points, home-sharing programs are implemented *in* the home through the emerging relationship between the matched *sharers*: provider and seeker (Schreter, 1984). As such, the arrangement is designed and managed by and for the sharers, with minimum agency intervention. The unique package of services each arrangement affords may provide for a wide spectrum of needs (e.g., from simply sharing housing costs to providing household services for those with functional limitations). Such arrangements may create new roles for elderly participants. The nature of the relationship can positively effect the ability of frail older persons to remain in the least restrictive living environment. In addition, housesharing can provide financial assistance and companionship in a familiar and comfortable setting.

In spite of the prominence awarded to shared housing, very little systematic research has been done on the topic. Of those studies which have sought to measure various characteristics of home-sharing programs, sample sizes have generally been small, making it difficult to perform tests of statistical significance. The present study examines the homesharing arrangements of Project MATCH, to begin to assess the success of such arrangements in meeting the needs and expectations of those involved. Among the issues examined are:

1. the demographic characteristics of persons who participate in homesharing programs,

2. the household and daily maintenance service needs which can be met by homesharing,
3. the interpersonal factors and environmental conditions which can contribute to the satisfaction or lead to the dissolution of matches,
4. the level of intimacy which can develop between partners and what accounts for differences, and
5. appropriate basis by which to classify matches.

DATA AND METHODOLOGY

Data Source

Data for this study is based on the experiences of 144 past and continuing participants of Project MATCH, a homesharing program based in San Jose, California. The program, began in 1977, is the oldest house-sharing service in the United States. It is administered by a private non-profit agency that arranges potential matches for seniors and other adult residents of the Santa Clara County. In 1981, the program was awarded the affordable housing award from the State of California. In its first one and one-half years, Project MATCH placed 400 seniors. By June 1986, almost 7,009 persons had been "matched." The project arranged sharing for 1,049 persons during 1982, providing a large subject pool available for analysis. The program has expanded to include other age groups and thus allow for intergenerational matches (where partners' ages differ by more than ten years).

Project MATCH is based primarily on a hybrid referral/counseling model (Dobkin, 1983). Potential clients call the agency and make an appointment for a personal interview with a housing counselor. At the time of the interview, a client intake, participation agreement and consent form are used as a basis to gather information. During the intake/screening period, clients are advised in terms of what to realistically expect from a shared housing arrangement. Counselors then search for referrals with complementary needs and compatible preferences. Currently, there is no fee to clients, although small donations ($5 for providers and $3 for seekers) are requested when possible.

Once the clients are interviewed and potential matches have been found, referrals are made by contacting each client by telephone and directing them to arrange a meeting time with their potential partner. After this initial meeting between potential partners, Project MATCH contacts each client to ascertain their respective reaction. If the match is arranged, a match certificate is signed. Participants are assisted in setting up rules, contracts, and written agreements if they choose. Follow up is provided after one, three, and six months from the time the arrangement is made, and then every six months, up to two years. For matches providing live-in service arrangements, follow up is done every month.

Data Collection

The sample group was selected randomly from the project's file of matches arranged between July 1, 1982 and November, 1983. In addition, seven matches were selected from the prior year for qualitative purposes. Since only providers' addresses are maintained in the roster and seekers who were no longer matched seldom left a forwarding address, it was not possible to locate most seekers once they left the homesharing project. As a consequence, 74 percent (107) of the 144 respondents were providers and 26 percent were seekers.

Information was gathered through the administration of a 28 page questionnaire over the telephone. Questions focused on the respondents' characteristics and the microlevel of interaction during the match. In addition, respondents were asked corresponding details concerning their partners. Standard questions were asked concerning health and mobility. Portions of several surveys were left incomplete as a result of respondents inability or refusal to answer questions.

SURVEY RESULTS

Characteristics of Sharers

Among those interviewed, 82 percent of all sharers, both providers and seekers, were women. Other studies (Howe, Robins and Jaffe, 1984; Pritchard, 1983) have supported this finding that homesharing programs disproportionately attract women. By contrast, the age composition varies significantly among different programs depending on the target population, location and housing market. The sample studied here ranged in age from 24 to 96 years, with an average age of 65 years. Providers tended to be older than seekers; 70% of providers were over age 60 as compared to only 59% of the seekers (see Table 1).

Respondents were also questioned about their ethnicity, marital status, employment status, income and health status. The majority of those sampled were Caucasian. Expectedly, widowers and divorcees were more often providers than seekers, while singles showed the reverse tendency. Also as expected, given the age of the respondents, most were retired: almost 70% of providers and 51% of seekers. Many other seekers appeared to be in transitory roles, 19% were unemployed and 5% were students. Seventy-eight percent of respondents were living on fixed incomes and over half (62%) of the subjects had monthly incomes under $600.

The health status of subjects was defined by a composite score based on: (1) the number of doctor visits in the last year, (2) the number of days spent in the hospital in the last year, (3) self-appraised health status (poor to excellent), (4) the extent to which health problems were reported to interfere with "doing things," and (5) number of ambulation limitations including walking, climbing stairs, boarding a bus, and using a walker or wheelchair. These five variables were entered into a factor analysis (see Table 2) to test for internal validity and to generate factor scores. The resulting factor loading revealed a high level of internal validity, and therefore supported the use of the five variables.

Factor scores were then generated and the resulting range of scores was divided into thirds to define respondents as either *nonfrail, slightly frail* or *frail*. The respondents falling into the *frail* category exhibited more than three ambulatory problems (55% of the *frail* had four such problems), as compared with 0 to 1 reported for the *slightly frail*. The *non-frail* respondents reported no ambulatory problems. As expected, due to the physical requirements of seeking housing, a higher proportion of providers (35%) were frail as compared to seekers (22%).

Table 1 - Characteristics of Sharers

	Percent of Respondents (N=144)	Provider (N=107)	Seeker (N=37)
Age			
Under 45	10	9	11
45-59	18	15	27
60-74	49	49	49
75 and old	23	27	13
Ethnicity			
Caucasian	82	82	81
Hispanic	10	9	16
Black	5	6	3
Other	3	3	0
Marital Status			
Widowed, divorced or separated	83	86	73
Single	10	6	22
Married	7	8	5

Employment Status

Retired	64	69	51
Working full-time	14	15	11
Working part-time	8	8	8
Unemployed	6	2	19
Other	8	6	11
Fixed income: Yes	78	--	--
No	22	--	--
Monthly income: under $300	15	10	26
$300-$600	47	46	48
$601-$900	15	14	17
over $900	24	30	9

Health Status

Nonfrail	33	32	34
Slightly frail	35	32	44
Frail	32	35	22

7

Table 2 - Factor Analysis for Determining Frailty Index

ITEM	FACTOR LOADING
Doctors visit	0.589
Hospital days	0.638
Self-reported health	0.685
Health interferes with doing things	0.901
Ambulation limitations	0.859

Eigenvalue = 2.77

Nature of Arrangements

Demographic Characteristics of Matches

With regard to gender and ethnicity, individuals tended to be matched with partners with characteristics similar to their own. Sixty-one percent of the matches were male-male or female-female. Similarly, 83% of the matches involved individuals of the same ethnic/racial background. In contrast, intergenerational matches, where the age of the partners differed by more than 10 years, were frequent (60% of the matches could be defined as intergenerational.)

Motivation for Sharing

Overall, the primary reasons considered by both providers and seekers in deciding to homeshare were financial need (44%) and companionship (21%) (see Table 3). Pritchard (1983) and McConnell and Usher (1980) also identified these two factors as the most common in motivating people to houseshare. Frail subjects were more apt to share because of health care needs, help in the home or security, rather than companionship reasons.

Table 3 - Motivations for Sharing

PRIMARY REASON	% OF SAMPLE (N=141)	PROVIDER (N=107)	SEEKER (N=37)	FRAIL (N=42)	SLIGHTLY FRAIL (N=42)	NON FRAIL (N=43)
Financial needs	44	42	50	26	52	56
Companionship	21	23	14	12	24	26
Security	6	8	0	12	4	2
Help in the home	10	11	5	19	4	5
Health care	9	11	3	24	4	0
Other	10	5	28	7	11	12

9

Housing Type and Facilities Shared

One reason homesharing has recently gained attention is the increased use of available space that this housing alternative capitalizes on. It therefore was anticipated that providers were more apt to share because they had extra space in their residence. The data however revealed that only 20% of respondents identified their house as "too big." Sixty-four percent of the respondents were sharing a single family home. In 98% of the matches the residence contained at least two bedrooms; bedrooms were seldom a shared space. Communal spaces most often shared included kitchen facilities (95%), entrance (94%), living room (93%), and laundry facilities (92%). Bathrooms were shared in 53% of the matches.

Financial Arrangements

Four types of financial arrangements were established between sharers, including: (1) seeker pays rent only (61%), (2) seeker pays rent and provides service (11%), (3) seeker provides services only (11%), and (4) seeker receives wages and free rent for services (17%).

Service Provision and Exchange

One goal of this research was to determine whether household and daily maintenance needs were being met by housesharing. Subjects therefore were asked first to assess need (see Table 4). As would be expected, frail respondents indicated the highest service needs, with over half needing help with shopping, housework, and getting places, and almost all needing help with household chores.

Given these needs for services, the next question asked was whether they were being met by the housesharing arrangement. As indicated in Table 5, the majority of those who needed help with laundry, meals and housework did receive this assistance. However, those tasks which are less a part of the daily household routine, such as heavy household chores and helping getting around in and outside the house, were less apt to be provided.

Table 4 - Percent Indicating Need for Assistance with a Specific Task

SERVICE	TOTAL SAMPLE (N=131)	FRAIL (N=42)	SLIGHTLY FRAIL (N=46)	NON FRAIL (N=43)	CHI SQUARE	p
	%	%	%	%		
Household chores	42	88	28	14	51.49	.000
Shopping	24	59	13	2	41.09	.000
Housework	22	53	15	0	35.38	.000
Help getting places	24	61	13	0	47.55	.000
Meals	15	34	9	2	19.03	.000
Laundry	13	40	0	2	36.56	.000
Help getting around the house	5	15	0	0	13.65	.001

Table 5 - Number and Percentage of Those Needing Help Who Received Help From Partner*

SERVICE	TOTAL SAMPLE		FRAIL		SLIGHTLY FRAIL		NON FRAIL	
	N	%	N	%	N	%	N	%
Household chores	54	28	35	29	13	38	6	0
Shopping	31	42	24	42	6	50	1	0
Housework	28	71	21	62	7	100	0	0
Help getting places	26	35	20	40	6	17	0	0
Meals	19	84	14	79	4	100	1	100
Laundry	17	59	16	56	0	0	1	100
Help getting around the house	6	33	6	33	0	0	0	0

* Test of significance could not be performed since sample sizes were too small.

Problems in Homesharing

Homesharing relationships bring together two previously unintroduced individuals, each with their own personal histories, to share a common living environment. It is reasonable, therefore, to anticipate that some problems may arise, especially in relationships demand close interaction. It was hypothesized that personality problems would be the least resolvable, since they are not immediately alterable. Also, it was believed that rules would have a positive impact on limiting the number or increasing the resolution of problems.

Almost 40% of the respondents indicated no serious problems associated with their match. Contrary to our hypothesis, the number of problems reported by respondents was not significantly related to whether sharers had established clear rules. In fact, sixty-five percent of respondents who indicated no problems did not have rules.

Of those problems which were identified as moderate or serious, personality (31%), cooking (16%) and housework (15%) were reported most often. Privacy, one of the most important factors contributing to a sense of independence, was perceived as a problem by only 11% of the subjects.

The number of problems was not related to demographic and situational variables tested such as: (1) whether the match was intergenerational, (2) if the partners were of the same gender, (3) the financial arrangement of the match, or (4) the number of tasks which the respondent received or gave assistance.

It was also hypothesized that arrangements involving a frail sharer might be more problematic, especially with regard to personality incompatibilities and privacy, since these matches could entail greater levels of interaction between partners. The results suggest that the slightly frail were more apt to report a problem, and the nonfrail were least likely to do so, although there was some variation on particular items. For example, personality problems were least often reported by the nonfrail (26%), as compared to the frail (32%), but this pattern was reversed for privacy problems. A slightly lower incidence of privacy problems were reported by the frail compared to the nonfrail.

Among the 41 respondents (31% of the sample) who reported a

personality problem, 21% of those problems were resolved. Other types of problems were also resolved, including over half of the bathroom, privacy and division of labor problems. Cooking and housework problems were resolved the least often (10%).

Reasons given the dissolution of the match varied greatly. Some were not a reflection on the success of the match but rather resulted because a partner decided to move, or as a result of death or institutionalization. Reasons reflective of unsuitable matches included general incompatibility, conflict or unacceptable behaviors. No specific sharer/match characteristics appear to be related to the termination or continuance of the match.

Emerging Relationships

As noted, companionship often was mentioned as a motivation for housesharing. Further it is likely that where companionship is not an initial motivator, the close proximity of the housesharing environment may foster the growth of friendship. In this sample, 49% of the respondents reported that they had become "friends" or "close friends" with their partners over the course of the match; 41% reported that they could confide in their housemate on personal matters. In addition, 47% of the respondents indicated that they would be willing to care for their partner for at least a week if he or she became ill.

To investigate whether the degree of friendship was related to any identifiable characteristics of the matched pair, a strength of friendship index was developed. A score of "1" was assigned for each of the following conditions: (a) if the respondent perceived their partner as a "close friend" (as compared with, "acquaintance" or "friend"), (b) whether or not the respondent could confide in their partner and (c) if the partner would aid the respondent in case of an illness. Thus, the scale ranged from a low of "0," if no conditions were met, to a high of "3," if all conditions were met.

Characteristics, such as the respondent's frailty status; sameness in ethnic origin, gender or generation; and the primary reason for sharing did not show a relationship to the level of friendship. The friendship level expressed by respondents differed significantly only for the variable describing whether the respondent was still matched. Sixty-two percent of respondents who had a score of "0" on the friendship scale were no longer matched at the time of the study, as compared with 18% of those who scored a "3" on the friendship scale. The data revealed indicative trends for stronger friendship interactions when either fewer problems were reported or when more "somewhat" or "important" needs were met by sharing.

Satisfaction with the Match

In general, respondents to the survey were satisfied with the housesharing relationship. Almost half (48%) indicated they were "highly" satisfied, 34% were "moderately" satisfied and only 18% were "not" satisfied. In an attempt to obtain a more global measure of satisfaction, a composite score based on the following measures was constructed: (1) overall rating of satisfaction, (2) friendship scale, (3) number of problems identified in the relationship, (4) degree to which expressed needs were met and (5) whether the match satisfied the respondent's primary reason for housesharing. These five variables were entered into a factor analysis (see Table 6) to test for internal validity and to generate factor scores. The resulting factor loading revealed a high level of internal validity and supported the use of the five variables in a composite scale. Factor scores were then generated and the resulting range of

Table 6 - Factor Analysis for Determining Satisfaction Index

ITEM	FACTOR LOADING
Overall satisfaction	.733
Friendship scale	-.648
Number of problems	.585
Expressed needs met	-.603
Primary reason met	.720

Eigenvalue = 2.18

scores was divided into quartiles. To examine the most extreme cases, only the respondents scoring in the top and bottom quarter of this scale were extracted for analysis.

The analysis reveals a very similar relationship between satisfaction and the variable most related to friendship. Specifically, the level of satisfaction expressed by respondents was related positively for sharers who were still matched (chi-square = 18.42; P < .001). Seventy-three percent of those who were highly satisfied were still matched at the time of the survey as compared with 31% of those who reported low levels of satisfaction. The data also reveals indicative and significant trends for stronger levels of satisfaction when either fewer problems were reported or when more needs were met by sharing. Other sharer/match characteristics, such as the respondent's frailty status, the primary reason for sharing, or whether partners were of the same ethnic origin, gender or generation did not show a relationship to the level of satisfaction.

Arrangement Typology

In further examining the nature of the relationship between partners, an attempt was made to classify matches. Through a retrospective analysis of sharer/match attributes, an attempt was made to establish which of these are consistent in predicting the likely nature of the relationship to follow.

The first typology scheme investigated the predictability by the financial arrangement established. Based on correlational analysis, neither frailty, number of services provided nor friendship levels were significantly related to the financial arrangement established. In fact, only 26% of the frail respondents were engaged in a "wage and free rent" arrangement, while 41% of them participated in "pay rent only" situations. The relationship between services and financial arrangement is equally unclear. For instance, 48% of respondents in "pay rent only" matches provided their partner with assistance in at least one service. In almost 10% of these relationships, over 3 service tasks were provided without renumeration. Partners with a score of "0" on the friendship scale were most often (64%) in "pay rent only" matches; however 65% of respondents with a high level of friendship were also in relationships set up as "pay rent only." Thus, the data reveals that the description of matches is not predictable on the basis of the financial arrangement.

Based on these findings, an alternative variable for predicting the nature of emerging relationships was suggested, namely, the degree of service provision or exchange. It was hypothesized that matches might fall into three basic types.

These three theoretical typologies were operationalized as follows:

1. service free: no services given or provided by either partner;
2. service exchange: at least one service given by the respondent to the partner and at least one service given by the partner to the respondent and;
3. service dependent: at least one service which respondent identified as needing help with is provided by his or her partner.

It was hypothesized that the third type would be more apt to include frail respondents and take on more of an employer-caretaker nature than the previously described matches. Within this sample, 54% of all matches were of the service free type, 20% were service exchange and 26% were service dependent.

In the majority (72%) of either service free or service exchange matches, the seeker "paid rent only." In the service dependent matches, however, 31% of respondents "paid rent only" and 36% were involved in "wages and free rent matches." Most respondents (80%) whose primary reason for sharing was financial were involved in service free (54%) and service exchange (48%) matches. Furthermore, 85% of respondents who entered housesharing arrangements because of health care needs were engaged in service dependent matches.

Table 7 illustrates that, as hypothesized, the relationship between the three service provision typologies and the degree of frailty of the respondent was significant. As expected, nonfrail respondents were most apt to be in service free matches (74%), while frail respondents were most often in service dependent matches (48%).

Consistent with Jaffe's (1984) hypothesis, the data revealed a significant positive relationship between service typology type and levels of friendship. Satisfaction with match is also significantly

Table 7 - Service Typologies by Degree of Frailty*

	N	SERVICE FREE (%)	SERVICE EXCHANGE (%)	SERVICE DEPENDENT (%)
Nonfrail	43	70	28	2
Slightly frail	46	50	26	24
Frail	42	40	12	48

* (Chi-square = 25.00; P≤ .001)

related with the service typology arrangement. However, while the level of friendship was a factor in developing the satisfaction index it was not the strongest determinant variable (see Table 8), hence, it does not necessarily follow that satisfaction will exist in all matches where friendship is significant. Sharers engaged in matches where services were not commonly provided or exchanged reported lower levels of friendship and satisfaction than those in relationships where services were provided.

DISCUSSION

Data from the present study indicate that, overwhelmingly, housesharing participants are female; Caucasian; either widowed, divorced or separated; and on fixed incomes. The age distribution of respondents, while dependent on the target group of the specific program under consideration, ranged from 24 years of age to 96 years of age. Providers were generally older than seekers, a result accountable by individuals having acquired assets (i.e., housing) with increased years. The analysis also identified one-third of the respondents as frail.

Several household and daily maintenance needs were met by the housesharing arrangements. Specifically, meal preparation, housework and laundry were the common tasks that partners provided. Interestingly, while help with heavy household chores was needed by the greatest percentage of the respondents, it was the service least likely to be provided by the housesharing partner. This result may indicate that such tasks are either too much to ask from a partner or are provided by outside resources. Gaps in services which the home-sharing partner is unable or unwilling to provide can result in the early dissolution of matches unless other support programs are in place. This is an especially salient issue for referrals who are at risk of institutionalization. Counselors need to be aware of the degree of dependency some participants will impose on their partners so that perhaps other programs can supplement the home-sharing arrangement.

Most (55%) of respondents indicated no problems with their matched partner; however, 25% identified one moderate or serious problem and 20% had at least two problem areas. The most com-

Table 8 - Service Typologies by Friendship Scale and Satisfaction Level*

	N	SERVICE FREE (%)	SERVICE EXCHANGE (%)	SERVICE DEPENDENT (%)
Friendship Scale				
Low (value = "0")	65	75	9	15
Medium (value = "1 or 2")	57	40	28	22
High (value = "3")	22	32	32	36

* significant at the .05 level (Chi-square = 24.93 and significance = .000)

	N	SERVICE FREE (%)	SERVICE EXCHANGE (%)	SERVICE DEPENDENT (%)
Satisfaction Level				
Low (lowest quartile)	29	72	14	14
High (highest quartile)	30	23	23	53

* significant at the .05 level (Chi-square = 15.00 and significance = .001)

20

mon problems (31% of matches) identified were personality incompatibilities. Privacy was not a central problem. In fact, no sharer/match variable was inherently problematic. Whether or not rules were set-up did not affect the type of problems nor the number of problems experienced by respondents.

When respondents were asked about their level of satisfaction, over 80% indicated that they were either moderately or highly satisfied. Not surprisingly, their response was related to whether or not they were still matched. Other variables which influenced satisfaction included the level of friendship achieved, as measured by the friendship index, and the number of problems identified. When the satisfaction scale was cross tabulated with the three service arrangement typologies, a significant relationship was identified. Sharers involved in matches where services were not provided nor exchanged, "service free" arrangements, reported lower levels of satisfaction as compared with respondents who exchanged services or were dependent on their partner for assistance.

Housesharing relationships are often a source of friendship and intimacy. Streib (1984) raises the issue of whether or not shared living arrangements represent genuine families. Based on his study of group homes, he suggests that such arrangements differ from natural families for a variety of reasons, such as certain kinds of foibles which may not be tolerated and the tendency of sharers to withdraw from the obligation during difficult times such as illness. Previous studies concerning such issues have concluded that older homeowners do not view their matches as a social context conducive to intimacy (Usher and McConnell, 1980). Contrary to this conclusion, almost half of the present sample indicated moderate to strong levels of friendship and 41% reported that they could confide in their partners on personal matters. Furthermore, half of the respondents said that they would be willing to care for their partner if they became ill for at least a week. This suggests that while homesharing arrangements fall short of family obligation, they nevertheless can develop far beyond the notion of strangers occupying a common living space.

The authors also sought to develop an appropriate typology which would categorize matches and, hence, characterize sharers. An appropriate typology would allow agency personnel to more effectively refer compatible clients and provide a realistic description of what to expect from the homesharing relationship. Intake forms often inquire about the financial arrangement the prospective sharer wishes to have. As the data shows, the financial arrangement, established during the contractual phase of matching before sharers move in together, is not representative of the relationships which later emerge.

As an alternative, matches were segregated on the basis of the type of service arrangement which emerged. A previous study by Jaffe (1984) identified three distinct kinds of role relationships, independent, mutual exchange, and total care, based on the level of impairment and subsequent degree of dependency of the elderly resident and the sense of control over the household. Independent matches characteristically had residents with no health problems who generally needed minimal assistance with heavy chores or home maintenance: seekers generally paid rent. Total care relationships involved residents with severe health problems and multiple disabilities: seekers were either the primary care provider or one member of a support system, which included professional nursing care during the day. These residents were quite dependent and logical candidates for nursing home care. Preliminary evidence by Jaffe (1984) suggests that in total care matches relationships tended to take the form of family-like models. In between these extremes were mutual exchange matches. Here, seekers were expected to provide services like shopping, preparing meals, vacuuming and doing laundry in exchange for room and board.

The service exchange typology presented in this research offers alternative interpretations to those presented by Jaffe. The analysis here suggests that the above characterization of matches is not clear. Jaffe argues that housesharing relationships are dictated primarily by health. However, while this research found a strong relationship between the type of service provision and exchange and the degree of frailty, it was not a one-to-one relationship. Approximately 40% of the *frail* respondents in this research were living in service free housesharing arrangements; an additional 12% were living in service exchange arrangements. This suggests that even an older person who is rather severely impaired has some valid choices in the housesharing arena and is not limited to a dependent role.

Furthermore, those who are in a service dependent relationship are not necessarily powerless in accepting an unsatisfying living arrangement because of their physical disabilities. In fact, those respondents living in service dependent relationships were found to be among the most satisfied, had high levels of friendship with their partners and were involved in matches of longer duration.

CONCLUSION

This research, supports a growing literature suggesting that although not a panacea for all housing problems, housesharing may be a viable housing alternative for a wide variety of older adults (e.g., Schreter, 1985). It may provide financial assistance and/or companionship in a relatively independent environment or it may provide needed household services and the opportunity to live at home for frail older persons. Respondents in this study most often stated financial motivations for participating in homesharing. Given this and the relatively minimal staff intervention time, homesharing should be promoted as an affordable housing alternative by community groups and non-profit housing developers. Furthermore, it has been shown that housesharing may lead to the development of new opportunities for interaction and may contribute to the friendship network of older and frail sharers. With regard to matching referrals effectively, agency personnel must inquire as to the willingness of clients to participate in different service arrangements, regardless of the financial arrangement. In addition, given the significant proportion of frail persons involved in homesharing, and the potential for disability among more healthy sharers, increased attention should be placed on typing them into community based long-term care systems and providing adequate agency backup that responds to their changing needs.

The analysis presented in this paper also raises a number of additional issues that require further investigation, such as the relationship between the establishment of rules and problems, as well as factors that affect the satisfaction and the duration of matches. In addition, the role of housesharing as part of the informal service network needs additional exploration. Such research would be aided by a longitudinally designed study that might better reveal the intricacies of these dynamic relationships.

REFERENCES

Dobkin, L. (1983). Shared Housing for older people: A planning manual for match-up programs. Philadelphia, PA.: Shared Housing Resource Center.

Howe, E.; Robins, B. and Jaffe, D. (1984). Evaluations of Independent Living's HOMESHARE Program, Madison, Wisconsin: Department of Urban and Regional Planning, University of Wisconsin, Madison.

Jaffe, D. (1984). The social relations of housesharing. Unpublished paper presented at the Annual Scientific Meeting of the Gerontological Society of America, November, 1984.

McConnell, S.R., & Usher, C.E. (1980). Intergenerational house sharing. Los Angeles: Andrus Gerontology Center, University of Southern California.

Pritchard, D.C. (1983). The art of matchmaking: A case study in shared housing. *Gerontologist, 23,* 174-179.

Schreter, C. (1984). Room for rent: Home sharing with nonrelated older Americans. (Doctoral dissertation, Bryn Mawr College, 1983). *Dissertation Abstracts International, 44,* 2250A.

_____ (1985). Advantages and disadvantages of shared housing, *Journal of Housing for the Elderly,* 3, 121-137.

Streib, G.F., Folts, E., & Hilker, M.A. (1984). *Old homes-New families: Shared living for the elderly.* New York: Columbia University Press.

Chapter 2

Supporting the Independence
of Elderly Residents
Through Control Over Their Environment

Ellen Feingold
Elaine Werby

SUMMARY. Increasing loss of control over one's life is associated with reduced independence and wellbeing in the elderly. A housing organization tries to prolong the independence of its residents by reinforcing the sense of competence endangered by age associated deterioration. Competence is enhanced by providing residents with genuine control over their lives and through access to real choices in necessities, in social contacts, in services and facilities. Choice and control are supported even at the cost of some increased resident risk-taking. A case study is presented showing the failure of a well-designed meals program without sufficient opportunity for choice and control. The paper concludes by citing conflicts which result from this approach, both for staff, internally, and externally with other community organizations which expect elderly to be cared for.

INTRODUCTION

Fear of loss of control over one's environment is often mentioned by the elderly. The loss of control is identified with loss of independence, something most elderly feel strongly about. Findings from

Ellen Feingold is Executive Vice President, Jewish Community Housing for the Elderly, 30 Wallingford Road, Boston, MA.

Elaine Werby, MSW, is Associate Professor, College of Public and Community Service, University of Massachusetts at Boston, Boston, MA.

research conducted among institutionalized elderly (Rodin and Langer, 1977; Mercer and Kane, 1979) as well as findings from a study of elderly living in retirement communities suggest a relationship between an enhanced perception of control and a sense of well-being. Slivinske and Fitch (1987) report that by the end of their study in a retirement community, ". . . individuals who had received control-enhancing interventions (classes in stress management; nutritional awareness; immediate environment; self-responsibility; physical fitness and spirituality) experienced significantly greater improvement in their level of perceived control and of wellness than members of the control group."

While the concept of control has been investigated in various settings under different research protocols, some practitioners are utilizing the concept as the framework for program design. This article describes how a housing management organization has formulated an approach to managing housing for the elderly using the concept of control as a central element in enhancing independence of residents as they age in place. The authors also discuss the costs and conflicts in carrying out this approach.

ORGANIZATION

Jewish Community Housing for the Elderly owns and operates five developments, now three to sixteen years old, with a total of 934 apartments. The three largest buildings with a total of 710 apartments are sited together in a Boston neighborhood. The two smaller buildings are on separate suburban sites. All the buildings were financed through state and federal low-income housing programs; only 24 units are occupied by families above low or very low income. Apartments are small, with the majority efficiency or one-bedroom units. Thirty-eight apartments are specially equipped for wheelchair accessibility. Each apartment has a full kitchen. All buildings have a variety of community areas but are not what is commonly known as "congregate housing." Average age of the close to eleven hundred residents is 80 and the median income is under $6,000.

JCHE's primary role is that of houser, to provide good, safe, affordable housing which means low rent, safety from outside physical dangers and security in personal physical or medical emergencies. The buildings are well-maintained, attractive, with ample community spaces which help create a pleasant, active and caring environment.

JCHE's mission is to provide housing and the housing-related services and facilities which support the ability of independent elderly persons to care for themselves. Management believes that the best way to prolong independence is to reinforce the sense of competence which is endangered in an elderly person as his or her real physical and mental powers diminish.

Competence is enhanced by exercising control over one's life and having access to choices. To support and enhance independence, the things people need, the necessities, must be available; a range of services and facilities must be available and accessible; real choices in social contacts as well as services and necessities must be possible. Real choices allow people whose strengths are ebbing to continue to exercise control over their lives, to demonstrate to themselves that they are still competent. The concept of competence described by Kupers and Bengstrom (1984) most closely resembles management's view.

ENHANCING CONTROL

A *major* factor in enhancing the residents' ability to keep control over their own lives is the Section 8 rent subsidy system through which residents pay just thirty percent of their adjusted income for rent with the federal government paying the remainder. This system allows the resident to retain seventy percent of income *in cash* after paying for rent and medical expenses. This is a *fundamental* source of independence: cash for the other things one needs, including food, clothing, transportation, and the things that make life worth living, like presents for the grandchildren. *Having cash is a basic necessity for having choice.*

Access to choice among services is a second important element of control. Here JCHE plays an active role in ensuring that residents have access to a range of services. To provide the service delivery system, JCHE acts as organizer, broker, negotiator and advocate, working with the responsive network of public and private social service and health agencies available in the Greater Boston area.

Jewish Family and Children's Service (JF&CS) provides onsite case management, family counseling, individual casework, home health and homemaker services. The Visiting Nurse Association and other agencies are also involved in at-home service delivery. Similar social services are also provided off-site by hospital social work departments, as well as community agencies such as the Chinese social agencies which serve the Chinese residents. Residents are free to select the service and agency which best fits their physical, emotional and cultural needs.

As part of the general program of group services in the buildings, health professionals regularly provide health care information and some screening, such as blood pressure and dental checks. The City of Boston provides hearing and vision clinics. Management's role and emphasis is on providing residents with information and access. Residents are free to participate in the health information and screening sessions, and many do take advantage of them. Others, free to choose, prefer to get their information and health checks privately at a hospital clinic or through their private physicians.

Social group activities are planned by the residents with staff support. The variety of activities appeals to the diversity of the residents, though many residents are not comfortable in the group activities and prefer to make their own social arrangements. Again, Management's role and emphasis is on insuring that all residents are aware of activities and are welcome to participate if they so choose.

Access to and choice for food shopping is provided by a "shopper's bus" which takes residents to local supermarkets, and by a small grocery store in each building which is stocked with all the necessities, including fresh vegetables and dairy products. Finally, a limited transportation program is available for those residents who need and choose this assistance.

Lawton (1985) characterized this pattern of service delivery as a ". . . patchwork of service," and described it as a ". . . relatively unplanned and uncoordinated . . . service package." In contrast to this image, JCHE's resident services staff maximizes coordination within the service delivery system through regular case conferences with its principal provider, JF&CS, and conscientious development of collegial relationships with all service providing agencies and their staff members.

CASE STUDY

It is the availability and accessibility of these varied services which provide residents with choice, control, and thus independence. When management's programming has not provided residents with choice and thus a sense of control, the program has failed. The dinner program in one of JCHE's buildings is a case in point.

The original intent in providing this service was to assure residents of a well-balanced diet and an opportunity for regular socialization. For these reasons, as well as cost factors, the program was mandatory, with a monthly payment which, at the outset, was affordable by all residents. It was assumed that inasmuch as residents accepted the mandatory dinner program as part of their tenancy, the major issue management would encounter would be to keep the program attractive.

Dinner was served restaurant style in an attractive dining room with small tables, a serving staff, real china, flowers, menu choices, and other details intended to create a pleasant ambiance. Despite this careful planning, problems emerged immediately. It soon became clear that, for operating as well as social reasons, seating had to be assigned. Every table had to be filled. Unpopular residents had to be accommodated. Serving the menu chosen by the resident the previous day required him or her to be in the same seat.

The assignment of seating not only created a more institutional atmosphere, but, more importantly, it robbed residents of choice of dinner companions and the freedom to be independent at the central event of the day.

In addition to the seating problem, management had overlooked other aspects of the program which robbed residents of control. Residents could not choose *when* to eat. Residents could not choose to eat privately, either occasionally or regularly, unless willing to forfeit their payment for the meals. Low-income residents in particular felt robbed of the opportunity to accept outside dinner invitations, including those from family, because they felt that would be wasting a meal for which they had already paid in the monthly payment. Residents with physical disabilities which affected their ability to eat neatly could not preserve their dignity by eating privately if they chose. Robbed of choice and thus control, women, the majority of residents, received a message that they were no longer competent to cook for or feed themselves.

JCHE's experience, not unlike the findings by Regnier et al., (1981), was that the mandatory aspect of the program became the focus of hostility, resentment, and ultimately so much rejection that it had to be discontinued. In meeting what was thought at the time to be the needs of the residents (after all, why would they choose to live in a building with a mandatory dinner program if they didn't want it?), management was taking away the opportunity for them to care for themselves, to make choices, to exercise control, to be independent.

In place of the mandatory dinner program, JCHE now provides in each building but one an informal "deli" or "buffet" where residents can buy prepared food, either to eat in an informal cafe environment or to take upstairs to their apartments. The accessibility and availability offered by this service provides real choice for the resident who remains in control of what, when and where he or she prefers to eat on any given day.

COSTS AND CONFLICTS

Other housing management organizations may provide a similar menu of services for their residents. JCHE does not claim that either its role in providing the services or access to them or even the array of services itself is unique. What perhaps does distinguish its operation is the clear explication of its philosophy and management approach.

JCHE has carefully delineated its primary role as houser. Within that definition it sees its responsibility as fostering and maintaining an environment which supports the independence of its residents as they age. Rather than taking on the necessary caregiving services directly, JCHE has elected to assist residents with the organization of their care and support as needed, from their social and family networks and from area social service agencies. In carrying out this function, whether as organizer, broker or advocate, management emphasizes the importance of availability, access and choice to enhance residents' sense of control and thus their independence.

To make this concept workable, JCHE has involved its entire staff in its implementation. All staff, from the administrators and resident services providers through the maintenance and grounds staff must be committed to a system which puts a premium on offering opportunities for choice and control. Staff are selected as much for their interest in participating in such a system as their specific skills. Much effort goes into in-service training which instructs staff how its actions in almost any situation can be utilized either for staff convenience and management control, or to enhance resident choice and control of his or her environment.

Explication and the carrying out of this philosophy has great benefits to residents, but it is not without its costs to the organization. It can cause real problems and conflicts.

The first conflict is between the organization's view of itself as caring and supportive against the need to allow residents the right to personal independence, even if this results in the resident taking less than optimum physical care and precaution about him or herself.

This conflict can cause substantial internal conflict for each staff member. The organization places great emphasis on its humanity, and it asks its staff members to be caring, helpful and supportive individuals and to exersize judgment in interacting with its residents. But it also challenges staff members to hold back on their caring, protective impulses in order to permit support for resident choice, control and independence, even when this produces some measure of personal risk to the resident.

Second, the implementation of this philosophy sometimes puts the organization at odds with the community and the community's expectation of a caring housing organization. To some extent, this reflects the community's persistent misunderstanding of the nature of independent housing, and its confusion with a nursing home. Beyond that, however, the community expects a caring housing organization to take care of its residents, to protect and serve dependent persons, rather than to strive to prolong and enhance independence. Thus, JCHE needs to articulate to the community at large the concept of control as a central element in maintaining the independence of its elderly residents.

CONCLUSION

Management of housing for the elderly should reflect and respond to the unique issues and concerns of its population. This article describes how one housing organization has approached this task. Management operations are designed to support a sense of competence and independence among its residents. Through providing residents with access and choice for services and activities, residents' control over their own lives is enhanced, and their real independence is strengthened.

REFERENCES

Kupers, Joseph A. and Bengtson. (1984), Perspectives on the Older Family. *Independent Aging*. Quinn, W. and Hughston, G., Eds. Rockville, MD. Aspen Systems Corp.

Lawton, M.P., Moss, M. & Grimes, M. (1985), The Changing Service Needs of Older Tenants in Planned Housing, *Gerontologist*, 25, p. 258-264.

Mercer, S. & Kane, R.A. (1979), Helplessness and Hopelessness among the Institutionalised Aged: An Experiment. *Health and Social Work*, 4, 91-116.

Regnier, V. & Gelwicks, N. (1981), Preferred Supportive Services for Middle to Higher Income Retirement Housing, *Gerontologist*, 26.

Rodin, J. & Langer, E. (1977). Long-term Effects of a Control-Relevant Intervention with the Institutionalized Aged. *Journal of Personality and Social Psychology*, 35, p. 897-902.

Slivinske, L.R. & Fitch, V.L. (1987). The Effect of Control Enhancing Interventions on the Well-being of Elderly Individuals Living in Retirement Communities. *The Gerontologist*, 27:2, p. 176-180.

Chapter 3

Living Arrangements
and Informal Social Support
Among the Elderly

Andrew Wister

SUMMARY. One of the most pervasive patterns in living arrangements observed among today's elderly has been the increasing propensity to live alone. This paper assesses the extent to which living
alone, living with a spouse, or living with others (no spouse present)
affects several dimensions of informal social support. The data for
this study are from a 1983 survey focusing on living arrangement
choices among elderly persons living in London, Ontario, Canada.
Overall, living arrangement is considerably more important as a determinant of instrumental support than social contact. Elders choosing to live alone appear to sacrifice some degree of mutual exchange
for privacy and independence. They also tend to rely on friendship
to a greater extent than married elderly or those who co-reside with
others. Implications for support services and changes in the family
are discussed in the context of living arrangement selection in later
life.

During the last few decades, patterns of non-institutional living
among older persons have changed dramatically. It is well docu-
mented (see for example, Kobrin, 1976; Soldo, 1981; Thomas and

Andrew Wister, PhD, is Professor, Sociology Department, University of Waterloo, Waterloo, Ontario, Canada N2L 3G1.

This paper is based on data that was collected with the support of a research
grant (#492-82-0034) provided by the Social Sciences and Humanities Research
Council of Canada. The writing of this paper was supported by post-doctoral
fellowships funded by the Manitoba Health Research Council (#6533) and the
Social Science and Humanities Research Council (#492-84-8002).
The author wishes to thank Bill Forbes for his helpful comments.

33

Wister, 1984) that the most noteworthy change has been a substantial increase in single person living. It has been argued that the composition of a household may contain important implications for availability of informal support (Fletcher & Stone, 1980; Treas, 1977) and for the utilization of health and other social services (Wan & Odell, 1981). However, research has not made clear to what extent and under what circumstances the various forms of social support are affected by the living arrangements of older persons.

Generally, the social relevance of living arrangements for patterns of informal support appears to rest primarily on the accessibility of a spouse, other family members, or sometimes non-kin and the resultant quantity and quality of support. Among elderly who have children, those who live alone are as likely as those in larger households to experience some sort of contact with adult children (Shanas, 1978; 1980). However, the relationship between family members living within the same household may be fundamentally different from a qualitative point of view. For example, social contact and affective types of support (often tied to social contact) can be obtained at a distance with greater ease than instrumental forms of support. Research on the various forms of informal support (such as family/non-family, peer/intergenerational, affective/instrumental, etc.) and their effectiveness emphasize the need to recognize several dimensions of support (Chappell, 1983). This suggests that living with a spouse, with other kin or alone may entail different and mutually exclusive patterns of support.

Living in a multiple person household represents a milieu that is potentially conducive to continuous care and greater amounts of interaction and exchange (Fletcher & Stone, 1980). In particular, those elderly who are in an intact marital relationship are often able to maintain independence in the face of declining health through mutual support (Treas, 1977). Although the presence of a potential non-spouse caregiver in the household does not necessarily denote the adoption of such a role, this arrangement usually provides sufficient conditions for daily help among those requiring such assistance. Older persons living alone may often receive adequate amounts of social contact and instrumental support from outside the household (Cantor, 1980), but at some level of need options may be limited and a decision is forthcoming as to living arrangement modification. This suggests that the timing of key life cycle events during the latter stages of life (such as role loss, health problems, widowhood, etc.) plays an integral role in the pattern of need experienced by the elderly individual by affecting their competence to cope with daily living (Ferraro, 1984) and may also directly alter aspects of the support network.

It is clear from the previous discussion that the causal link between living arrangements and social support is confounded by the dual nature of the relationship. For example, the presence of adequate support from outside the household may create the option to live alone, while conversely, living arrangements may determine the type and amount of support received. Working within the limitations of cross-sectional data, it is argued that an analysis of patterns of informal social support across living arrangements will serve as an important starting point for further research.

This paper will attempt to assess the extent to which living arrangements influence patterns of family social contact, peer social contact and instrumental types of informal support. An indicator of perceived health status and the demographic variables age and sex will, in combination, reflect life-cycle change associated with patterns of need and coping ability and will also be incorporated into the analysis.

METHODOLOGY

The data for this study are from a 1983 survey focusing on living arrangement choices among elderly persons living in London, Ontario. The sample entails 454 respondents 65 years and over living in noncollective households, selected by means of a stratified random sample by age and sex.

Three measures of informal support were used in the analysis, including peer social contact, family social contact, and level of informal support. The first support measure involves an additive scale of the number of times per month that an individual sees family members socially, representing a measure of family social contact. The second measure entails a scale comprising the number of times per month that respondents see friends socially. It is recognized that some social contact may not be supportive but that, in general, a relationship does exist between frequency of contact and affective support. The other measure designates instrumental informal support. Here respondents were coded as having some help or no assistance from family and friends on the following 13 activities or tasks: housekeeping, shopping, meal preparation, laundry, bathing, taking medicine, transportation, social activities, banking, other financial matters, gardening, snow removal, and other heavy work around the home. This allowed for the creation of a 13 point task specific scale depicting instrumental informal support.

The central independent variable of interest is living arrangement and is divided into three categories including: (1) living alone (n = 159, 35%), (2) living only with a spouse (n = 216, 46%), and (3) living with others besides a spouse (n = 50, 11%). Those living both with a spouse and others (n = 29, 8%) constitute a separate group and were eliminated from the analysis due to small numbers.

For peer social contact, living arrangement was represented by two dummy variables and included in a single multivariate analysis. However, since marital support was not included in the family contact variable or the instrumental support measure, a problem arises when comparing those living only with a spouse and those living with others (besides a spouse). For these support measures, it was therefore deemed necessary to divide the living arrangement variable into two dichotomies for separate analysis, where living alone is designated as the comparison group. Thus, living alone is juxtaposed with elderly living only with a spouse for one analysis, while placed against elderly living with others for a separate analysis. The former involves comparisons of support from only outside the household, while the latter entails support from inside as well as outside the household, if relevant. Ideally, it would be preferable to access measures of informal support from all members within the household as well as from outside the household and to include a greater number of living arrangement permutations.

The measure of health status used in this analysis involves a four point scale of perceived strength and mobility. Respondents judged themselves as being excellent, good, fair, or poor in terms of physical strength and ability to get around. Respondent's exact age and their gender were also included.

RESULTS

To determine the extent to which living arrangement affects the dependent variables, net of the other independent variables, hierarchical regression analyses were performed on the data. The variables age, sex, and perceived strength and mobility were entered into the equations in the initial step using a forced entry approach, followed by the living arrangement variables. The former set of variables reflect life cycle change and are viewed as preceding household status sequentially.

Assessment of the distributions of the three indicators of informal support indicates a tendency for a mild upward straggle resulting in skewed distributions. The strategy most commonly used to correct this problem and used to convert the above variables is the application of natural log transformations (Erickson and Nosanchuk, 1977). The regression analyses were repeated using the non-transformed variables as well, with only minor changes occurring in the betas and R squares. Only the former analysis will be presented in the ensuing discussion.

A. Frequency of Peer Social Contact

The regression analysis for peer social contact appears in Table 1. Living arrangement is coded into two dummy variables with living alone as the (omitted) comparison category. Only strength/mobility and the two living arrangement dummy variables (dummy 1 and dummy 2) display significant relationships with peer social contact. (betas = .108, −.193, and −.291, respectively). Together, these variables contribute to a weak-moderate R square (.092). Interestingly, living with others or only with a spouse entail lower levels of peer social contact than elderly living on their own, while taking into account the other independent variables. Maintaining frequent contact with friends appears to be a more important aspect of the lives of elderly living alone and may provide a key source of affective informal support. In addition, those who are healthier tend to experience greater levels of peer contact.

TABLE 1:   Multiple Regression of Peer Social Contact on Life Cycle Variables
           and Dummy Living Arrangement Variables

VARIABLE	PEER SOCIAL CONTACT	
	B	β
SEX	.082	.040
AGE	.003	.018
STRENGTH and MOBILITY	.109	.108*
DUMMY 1	-.590	-.193***
DUMMY 2	-.574	-.291***
INTERCEPT	1.843	
R^2		.092***

DUMMY 1 - spouse only = 1, living alone and with others = 0

DUMMY 2 - with others = 1, living alone and spouse only = 0

SEX - female = 1, male = 0

B - unstandardized coefficient

β - standardized coefficient

*p = .05

***p = .001

B. Frequency of Family Social Contact

The two regression analyses for the frequency of family social contact can be found in Table 2. In the first, elderly living only with a spouse are contrasted with those living alone. When the independent variables are entered into the equation, none of the beta coefficients exhibit a statistically significant relationship with family social contact. The proportion of variance explained is also small (R2 = .018). Whether an elderly individual lives only with a marital partner compared to living alone has little or no effect on the likelihood of experiencing social contact with kin members from outside the household.

When living arrangement consists of comparing elderly living with others (besides a spouse) against elderly living alone, different results emerge. In this case, only the living arrangement variable reveals a significant association (beta = .336; R2 = .140). Thus, whether an older person lives with others rather than lives alone means significantly greater amounts of contact with family mem-

TABLE 2: Multiple Regressions of Family Contact and Level of Instrumental Informal Support on Life Cycle Variables and Dichotomized Living Arrangement Variables

VARIABLE	FAMILY SOCIAL CONTACT		LEVEL OF INSTRUMENTAL SUPPORT	
	B	β	B	β
SEX	.096	.047	-.016	-.013
AGE	-.013	-.086	.019	.199***
STRENGTH and MOBILITY	-.049	-.048	-.254	-.399***
SPOUSE ONLY/LIVING ALONE	.176	.119	-.330	-.268***
INTERCEPT	2.640		-1.405	
R^2	.018		.404***	
SEX	.334	.109	.059	.027
AGE	-.019	-.123	.024	.225***
STRENGTH and MOBILITY	-.129	-.110	-.380	-.460***
WITH OTHERS/LIVING ALONE	.907	.336***	.544	.286***
INTERCEPT	2.428		-2.214	
R^2	.140***		.462***	

spouse only = 1, living alone = 0

with others = 1, living alone = 0

SEX - female = 1, male = 0

B - unstandardized coefficient

β - standardized coefficient

***p = .001

bers from both inside and outside the household. The moderate explained variance indicates that selecting to co-reside rather than live separately is of importance in affecting levels of family contact. It must be recognized, however, that choosing to live alone may not necessarily involve levels of contact with family members that are unsatisfactory or inadequate for the elderly individual, since these factors have not been measured.

C. Instrumental Informal Support

The measure of instrumental informal support assumes a 13 point task specific scale. The two regression analyses on this indicator of instrumental informal support are also presented in Table 2. Except for sex, the remaining independent variables including living arrangement (dichotomized into living only with spouse and living alone) display statistically significant beta coefficients in the first equation. Perceived strength and mobility is found to be the strongest predictor, followed by living arrangement and age. Elderly with lower perceived strength and mobility, who are older, and who live alone rather than with a spouse more likely receive outside assistance on the instrumental support scale. The advantages of having a marital partner present, which appears to facilitate greater amounts of mutual support from within the household, is apparent from these findings. Furthermore, the large proportion of explained variance (40 percent) suggests that these variables represent central determinants of instrumental informal support to the elderly.

The second regression on level of instrumental support, where living arrangement is dichotomized into living with others and elderly living by themselves, results in the same statistically significant independent variables and a large R square (.462). As well, the ranking of coefficients is identical to the previous regression analysis. While lower perceived health and being older means higher levels of instrumental support, those living with others rather than living alone experience significantly higher levels of this style of social support. However, this includes support from inside as well as outside the household. The proximity of potential support associated with coresidence appears to contribute to higher levels of helping than for elderly who live separately, even after controlling for perceived health status, age, and gender.

DISCUSSION

Overall, living arrangement is considerably more important as a determinant of instrumental support than of social contact. Regarding the latter, a propensity exists for those elderly living with others (besides a spouse) to experience relatively high levels of family social contact but low levels of peer social contact when contrasted with elderly living alone. Perhaps the tendency for seniors living with others to co-reside with kin increases the likelihood of social interaction with family members, while concurrently inhibiting friendship development to some extent. Conversely, those living by themselves are characterized as seeing friends frequently while being less likely than co-residers to see family members, suggesting that there may be some degree of substitution of peer for family affective support.

Compared to those who live alone, elders living in an intact marital relationship display an inclination for lower levels of peer social contact. This suggests that married seniors may require fewer friendships and less affective support from outside the household, probably because the intimate nature of the marital dyad adequately provides for most of these needs. Comparisons between married elderly and those living separately in terms of social contact with family members reveals no significant differences. It appears that elderly living alone, on average, do not live a life depicted by social isolation from their family, but rather, enjoy levels of family interaction similar to that experienced by married elderly, from outside the marital relationship. This finding supports work by Soldo (1981) and others showing that separate living does not necessarily imply a deterioration of family ties.

In contrast, when focusing on instrumental support, the life cycle indicators—age, and strength/mobility surface as potent explanatory variables in addition to living arrangement. As expected, becoming older and experiencing limitations in physical strength, and mobility tend to increase the likelihood of receiving instrumental informal support. Being female does not significantly alter this probability.

It is not surprising that those living with a spouse receive less assistance in daily living from outside of the household due to the prevalence of mutual assistance in home production and personal care from within the household. Our findings suggest that movement from a state of being married to a state of being widowed can represent a dramatic shift in terms of the accessibility of instrumental support. At this point, certain considerations are usually forced on the remaining spouse concerning meeting instrumental needs.

Selecting to live with others (besides a spouse) provides a social environment that is conducive to a strong support base for assistance on key tasks and activities linked to daily living. In comparison, those choosing to live alone are recipients of considerably less facilitation on these tasks. With the onset of age and the culmination of functional disabilities decisions are often forthcoming as to how one changes their physical and social environment to adjust to such conditions. Invariably, compromises must be made that often involve sacrificing preferred living styles for alternative arrangements which will at minimum allow for now-institutional living (Wister, 1985).

Several implications arise from these discussions. First, the propensity towards separate living styles appears to entail a concomitant movement away from informal instrumental assistance. This may be mitigated by the growth in functionally manageable single person living units in tandem with the availability of formal support within the community. Second, it is apparent that the movement towards separate living among older persons carries with it an inherent limitation regarding the accessibility of instrumental support. Recent interest in shared living styles and cottage flats appear to be valuable as alternative living arrangements with built-in support systems. Finally, although the trend has been a movement towards government and community responsibility for providing support to the elderly, our findings indicate that elders co-habiting with family members enjoy considerably greater levels of instrumental support. This suggests that governments might consider implementing significant tax breaks or other forms of financial support to families who subsume such responsibilities.

Further investigation into the extent to which living arrangements affect social support may benefit through the utilization of longitudinal research designs to untangle the causal links between these variables. There is also a need to incorporate measures of formal support into subsequent analyses in order to capture interaction or substitution between informal and formal sources.

REFERENCES

Cantor, M.H. (1980). "The informal support system: its relevance in the lives of the elderly." In E.F. Borgatta and N.G. McClushey (Eds.) *Aging and society: current research and policy perspectives*. Sage Publications, Beverley Hills, CA.

Chappell, N.L. (1983). "Informal support networks among the elderly." "*Research on Aging*," 5(1), 77-99.

Erickson, G.H. and Nosanchuk, T.A. (1977). Understanding data. McGraw-Hill Ryerson Ltd. Toronto, Canada.

Ferraro, K.F. (1984). "Widowhood and social participation in later life." *Research on Aging*, 6(4), 451-468.

Fletcher, S. & Stone, L.O. (1980). "Living arrangements of Canada's older women and their implications for access to support services." Unpublished paper, Statistics Canada, Ottawa.

Kobrin, F.E. (1976). "The fall in household size and the rise of the primary individual in the United States," *Demography*, 13(1), 127-138.

Shanas, E. (1978). "A national survey of the aged." Final report to the Administration on Aging. U.S. Department of Health, Education and Welfare, Washington, D.C.

Shanas, E. (1980). "Older people and their families: the new pioneers." *Journal of Marriage and the Family*, 40, 9-15.

Soldo, B.J. (1981). "The living arrangements of the elderly in the near future." In S. Kiesler, J. Morgan and V. Oppenheimer (Eds.) *Aging: Social change*. Academic Press, New York, N.Y.

Thomas, K. & Wister, A.V. (1984). "Living arrangements of older women: the ethnic dimension." *Journal of Marriage and the Family*, 46(2), 301-311.

Treas, J. (1977). "Family support systems for the aged, some social and demographic considerations." *The Gerontologist*, 486-497.

Wan, T.T.H. & Odell, B.G. (1981). "Factors affecting the use of social and health services among the elderly." *Aging and Society*, 1, 95-115.

Wister, A.V. (1985). "Living arrangement choices among the elderly." *Canadian Journal on Aging*, 4, 127-144.

Chapter 4

The Housing and Support Costs of Elderly with Comparable Support Needs Living in Long-Term Care and Congregate Housing

Leonard F. Heumann

SUMMARY. Congregate housing has been proposed as a substitute for institutionalization for elderly who do not require skilled nursing care, but who are too frail for conventional housing. Cost comparisons with long-term care have attributed exaggerated savings to congregate housing by employing data that fails to control for elderly with equivalent support needs in both facility types. This paper reviews past cost comparisons and presents new findings for elderly with comparable support needs. Different assumptions about age and capital cost of the facilities, method of reimbursement (public and private), and level of resident functional ability demonstrate cost savings attributable to congregate housing ranged from $300-$6072 per resident per year in 1985.

INTRODUCTION

The purpose of this paper is to determine if there are significant savings to the elderly and to governments, if elderly capable of assisted, independent living were to be provided congregate housing rather than accommodation in a long-term care facility.

Long-term care facilities include nursing homes and homes for

---

Leonard F. Heumann is Professor, Housing Research and Development Program, University of Illinois, at Urbana-Champaign.

45

the aged, facility designed to provide long-term care for the chronically frail and ill who are incapable of independent living. Over the years many of these facilities have adapted their policies to include elderly residents who are capable of assisted independent living. In part, this has been a response to the growing number of elderly without support and incapable of living in conventional housing. Depending on the local policy of long-term care facilities and the availability of support services in the community, most studies estimate that between 20 and 25 percent of the elderly living in long-term care facilities could live in the community (Booz, Allan and Hamilton, 1975; Butler, 1975; Deetz, 1979; Kistin and Morris, 1972; Lawton, 1979; Thompson, 1978; Townsend, 1962; U.S. House, 1976). This is a significant percentage given the growing proportion of the population surviving to old age, especially if these elderly can live at a lower cost, with greater dignity and functional independence in the community.

Congregate housing has been identified as a housing option that provides the level of assisted, independent living which could meet the needs of elderly with chronic functional disabilities who are still capable of maintaining an independent apartment with support assistance. A congregate housing facility provides independent apartments along with congregate dining, social lounges, laundry facilities, recreation spaces, and a secure barrier free environment. Residents live independently but receive at least one major meal served congregately per day, and have the option of receiving assistance with additional meals, housekeeping, personal care, transportation and other support services if and when it is needed. No professional nurse is stationed on-site in a congregate facility. The typical on-site staff includes only a building manager, janitorial service and occasionally a social organizer. Congregate meals can be cooked on-site or catered. When support services are required they are called in to provide support *at the margin of individual need*, rather than being provided institutionally. Elderly who require constant skilled surveillance or care would have to be transferred to a long-term care facility. However, studies of the elderly population indicate that of the approximately 20 percent with chronic functional dependencies, more than two-thirds can live out their lives with the level of assisted, independent living provided by congregate housing, while less than one-third require a long-term, dependent living arrangement (Heumann and Boldy, 1982).

Cost comparison between congregate housing and long-term care facilities presents a difficult and complex research problem. There are three basic reasons: first, the two types of facilities represent very different living environments (especially with regard to private accommodations); second, they represent very different support care alternatives (long-term care uses on-site staff while congregate housing relies heavily on visiting services); and third, as indicated above, 75 to 80 percent of the long-term care population on average, are too frail to live in congregate housing, yet their support costs are often difficult to separate from the 20 to 25 percent who can transfer to congregate housing.

PREVIOUS COST COMPARISON RESEARCH

Almost all of the previous research uncovered shows cost savings with congregate housing. However, most of the studies *do not* control for comparable services to elderly with comparable support needs, nor do they always compare full housing and support service costs in both facilities. As a result, cost comparisons are not always accurate and often falsely exaggerate the savings in congregate living or the costs in long-term care facilities.

Research by the International Center for Social Gerontology and testimony at a 1981 U.S. Congressional Hearing indicated that, in the mid-to-late 1970s, congregate housing was approximately 40 percent less expensive to provide on a monthly basis than intermediate nursing home care (Nachison, 1979; U.S. House of Representatives, 1981). Testimony from the San Antonio Housing Authority before a U.S. Senate committee looking into congregate housing indicates that meals, personal assistance and housekeeping could be provided for about $2-$5 per person per day (mid-1970 prices), compared to local nursing home costs of $25-30 per person per day (Nachison, 1979).

Because congregate housing was relatively new when these studies were conducted, the studies often relied on a single congregate facility and made comparisons with state or national data on the cost of long-term care without carefully controlling for factors such as the level of support needed and actual support received.

Comparing Federal Congregate Services to Long-Term Care

Under Title IV of the 1978 Housing and Community Development Act, Congress authorized a federal Congregate Housing Services Program (CHSP). The Act allowed HUD to grant 3-5 year contracts to Public Housing Authorities and housing sponsors for provision of meals and supportive services to elderly and handicapped residents who are at risk of institutionalization, or who are undergoing long-term recuperation from illness (Anderson, 1984; Neno, et al., 1985). By 1985 this "demonstration" program had funded 65 project sites around the country.

Preliminary findings in a recent article calculates government subsidies by taking the average cost per person per year for congregate services, adding the average yearly subsidy for apartment rentals by the U.S. Department of Housing and Urban Development, and subtracting average annual participant contributions. Converted to monthly averages these figures are $288 + $143 − $48 respectively, for a total cost of $383. This is compared to an average yearly government subsidy for skilled nursing home care, which converted to a monthly average of $1209 (Neno, et al., 1985, pp. 11-12). This produces an impressive monthly congregate housing government subsidy savings of $826, or over 300 percent. Once again, this type of analysis is not a direct comparison of elderly in each environment with similar support needs. The use of skilled care subsidies in nursing homes in this calculation is particularly suspect because it uses the most dependent elderly with highest support costs, and clearly people who could never live in congregate housing.

Studies by States with Congregate Housing Programs

There are currently 15 states with some form of congregate housing program (subsidizing services and/or construction and/or rent), legislation pending in one or more of these areas (Heumann 1985).

Most of these states are located along the east coast or in the mid-western portion of the country. Four of the oldest programs have conducted cost comparison studies between their program and long-term care.

A 1982 New Jersey program provides personal support services to frail elderly tenants living in subsidized housing facilities, and financial assistance to help these elderly tenants purchase services available through the program. Services are limited to two: at least one hot meal served in a group setting, and a combination of personal care and housekeeping service. Approximately 500 tenants were receiving this service in 1985 (New Jersey, 1984).

The New Jersey analysis only compared long-term care facility costs for these limited congregate services (no housing subsidy and only 1-2 meals per day), and used full intermediate nursing home care, which was called "the next most likely care available" (New Jersey, 1984, p. 2). The average daily congregate services in 1982-83 cost $6 (average tenant fee = $2.26, average subsidy = $3.74). Daily intermediate care costs for residents who could contribute some income was $41-$44 (New Jersey, 1984, p. 2).

In 1984 the state of Maine passed a permanent Congregate Housing Program amending a demonstration program begun in 1980. All housing facilities participating in the congregate service subsidy are existing federally subsidized low income elderly projects. The services include noon meals; housekeeping and personal care services (including assistance with other meals as needed), and visiting home health and case management services. Twenty-two percent of the participants are former nursing home or boarding house residents (Gardner, 1984).

In 1984, the costs at eight congregate facilities were determined using all services and fair market rents. Service costs were determined by available funding sources (state CHSP funds, tenant fees, etc.). These costs were compared to nursing homes and boarding homes. Based on the states' share of monthly costs, nursing homes cost $409; boarding houses, $367; and congregate housing, $100. Overall, monthly costs including federal subsidies and client share were $1263 for nursing homes, $650 for boarding homes, and $775 for congregate housing (Gardner, 1984, p. 6).

The study did not say what level of nursing care was being used in the comparison. The study concluded that congregate housing is very cost effective when compared with nursing home care and comparable in cost to boarding homes. Because the state share of costs is far less for congregate housing than for boarding homes, and the quality of congregate housing is perceived as far greater by state analysts, recent state policy has begun to curb the growth of nursing and boarding homes while working actively to increase the supply of congregate housing (Gardner, 1984, p. 7).

In 1977, the State of Connecticut created a Congregate Housing Program that provides grants and loans to housing authorities, housing development corporations and other approved corporations for the development and operation of congregate housing. As of April 1985, 124 units were in operation (Canale and Klinck, 1985, p. 5).

In 1984, Connecticut completed a cost effectiveness study comparing three congregate facilities (94 units) and state nursing homes. Total rent (including the annualized value of the state construction grant) and full services were calculated, and the weighted average cost per month was $645. Income from tenant contributions, federal service monies, and state DOH service and construction subsidies yielded a weighted average subsidy of $333 per month. This subsidy cost was compared to state Medicaid costs for similar low to moderate income individuals in nursing homes. After subtracting average client contributions and federal reimbursements, the state's subsidy was $678 per month for the average of all nursing homes in the study and $1178 for new long-term care facilities (Canale and Klinck, 1985, p. 69-70). Thus, the study yielded a state average subsidy per tenant month for nursing homes that was two to three and one-half times higher than for congregate housing.

The average annual cost to Connecticut for one nursing home bed is $10,200. The state Health Coordinating Committee estimates a need for 3400-5000 new nursing home beds by 1990 unless a major public commitment is made to develop a community alternative like congregate housing. They quote New York, Massachusetts, and Maine studies that found 17 percent, 20 percent, and 22 percent respectively of their congregate housing residents had previously resided in nursing homes. They also quote a National Health Service study that shows 64 percent of deinstitutionalized elderly require the housekeeping and meal assistance found in congregate housing (Canale and Klinck, 1985, p. 71-72).

Massachusetts has one of the oldest and largest state congregate housing programs. Begun in 1978, the program has 198 state-subsidized congregate housing units in place as of 1984 (Commonwealth of Massachusetts, 1985). An additional 1847 units have been funded or are under construction according to the 1984 annual report. Home care services and the congregate housing co-ordinator for each site are paid for by the Executive Office of Elder Affairs, while Medicaid eligible health service reimbursements come from the Department of Public Welfare (Commonwealth of Massachusetts, 1985; Molica, et al., 1984).

In June of 1984, the Massachusetts Executive Office of Elder Affairs completed a state-wide assessment of the Congregate Housing Program funded in part by the U.S. Administration on Aging, private foundations, and the State. Not only were costs for 114 residents of congregate housing directly examined, but 21 of these residents lived in nursing homes prior to moving to congregate housing, allowing for the first time, an accurate comparison of housing and support costs in both facility types. The study found that average nursing home costs for these 21 elderly was $1116 per month. The average congregate housing costs for the same 21 elderly was $880 per month or more than 20 percent less than the cost of nursing home care (Molica, et al., 1984, p. 93).

In addition, the study compared the cost to administer social and health support services to elderly living in congregate housing and in private homes or apartments. The study found that the average amount of homemaker hours was 25 percent fewer for congregate housing clients compared to community clients, primarily because of greater economy and efficiency afforded by the group living in congregate housing (Molica, et al., 1984, p. 94). There was no similar economy for visiting nurses or home health aids. The amount, type, and frequency of these services resulted in little difference in delivery cost to a congregate resident or elderly living in individual homes.

The study also found that a lack of congregate or equivalent housing, not the need for extensive nursing related care, was the reason why many elderly were placed in nursing homes (Molica, et al., 1984, p. 94). Sixteen percent of the residents sampled in the state funded congregate housing had been moved from nursing homes (Molica, et al., 1984, p. 103).

COST COMPARISON IN THE MIDDLE WEST

In 1985, the Illinois Housing Development Authority was interested in determining the differences in care delivery and cost of care for elderly *with comparable support needs/dependency* living in congregate housing and long-term care facilities in Illinois. Because Illinois has too few congregate facilities to produce an acceptable sample, sites were sampled from a universe made up of seven midwest states: Illinois, Iowa, Michigan, Minnesota, Missouri, Ohio, and Wisconsin (Heumann, 1985).

The 1985 study was also an extension, in part, of a 1975 study in Illinois of long-term care facilities which showed that virtually all skilled care residents in Illinois are properly housed and could not be moved to more independent environments; but 28 percent of the intermediate care and 78 percent of sheltered care residents entering long-term care facilities could also live in semi-independent housing in the community if proper facilities (such as congregate housing) were available (Booz, Allan, and Hamilton, 1975).

The 1985 study was designed to avoid the assumptions that limited the reliability and universality of the findings of previous studies reviewed above. First, previous studies compared only the difference in government subsidy, implying that the subsidies themselves cover similar costs and/or that nonsubsidized costs are equivalent. As will be shown, this is not the case; congregate housing, for example, involves private support costs and daily living costs the resident incurs in maintaining a private apartment that are included in most long-term care subsidies. Second, the congregate housing costs used in previous studies are derived from the publicly managed or not-for-profit sponsored facilities eligible for the government congregate housing subsidy, while the long-term care costs are drawn from the full universe of facilities which serve public aid tenants, including private-for-profit facilities. This would not be a problem if all facilities incurred similar expenses, provided similar quality service and were reimbursed equally. However, these are all variable factors. Different facilities (public, not-for-profit and private) alter the ratio of public aid to private pay residents to meet their expenses. Private pay residents, in effect, subsidize public aid residents, but do so to different degrees in different facilities. Finally, by using very general cost figures for long-term care facilities, many of the previous studies include residents requiring far more costly and expensive health care and surveillance than could realistically manage a congregate living environment.

Methodology and Basic Site Characteristics

The 1985 Illinois study looks at all costs, subsidized and nonsubsidized, to the congregate housing and long-term care facility residents that are not clearly identical for residents of both facilities. It also identifies the universe of congregate and long-term care facilities that are comparable by identifying facility characteristics that explain variations in cost of operation and services. Facilities were selected for study that are representative of the norm on these characteristics. Finally, the range of support service dependency in congregate housing was identified and costs derived by interviews with site managers. This was followed by interviews with long-term care facility staff where costs were derived for residents with levels of support service dependency comparable to the congregate housing population.

Because of the depth of cost analysis and the need to choose both long-term care and congregate housing sites with comparable residents, the sample universe had to be very carefully defined and stratified, and the study sites had to be limited to 14 (7 of each). In addition, it was necessary for facility owners to open their books and reveal detailed costs and charges. A high refusal rate was correctly anticipated, especially among for-profit facilities. Even after initial agreement and an indepth site visit, one for-profit long-term care facility sampled refused to release key cost figures and had to be dropped from the study reducing the long-term care sites to six.

All facilities studied were limited to cities of 20,000 population or larger, located in counties defined as urban in the 1980 Census. This was necessary because of the significant differences in housing and support service character and cost, and support service availability between urban and rural areas, and the fact that the relatively small sample of sites being studied could not represent both urban and rural cost comparisons.

Congregate Housing Sample

In addition to the urban focus, eligible congregate facilities were limited to single buildings, with private apartments for residents (bedroom or studio style, private lavatory with bath or shower and private kitchen area), no entry fee or endowment, a minimum package of congregate services and spaces (one hot meal daily served in congregate dining and provision for other homemaker and personal care services as needed), and basic barrier-free and security design. This is by far the most common style of congregate housing in the Midwest and eliminates wide variation in the amount and type of living space the residents receive and are required to maintain.

A total of 55 congregate facilities fitting the above criteria were identified. These were then stratified by two characteristics: ownership and facility size. Twenty-six percent of the sites were private for-profit with an average facility size of 152 units; 60 percent were not-for-profit private or religious affiliated owners, with an average facility size of 127 units; and 14 percent were government owned (public housing) with an average size of 122 units. The facilities sampled were limited to a size range of 75 to 225 units to control for economies-of-scale in management and support service costs and sampled in proportion to he three ownership types. Due to lack of cooperation with private for-profit owners, only one site instead of two were sampled and an extra private not-for-profit owner was included.

Following selection, the congregate facilities were visited prior to any sampling of long-term care facilities in order to first establish the range of functional disability that can be accommodated in congregate housing. Each site was visited, operating functions and accommodations observed, a formal survey administered to the management, expenses incurred and income received assembled from facility books and staff (as appropriate), and resident expenses assembled from staff and visiting support service providers. The seven sites represented 1035 units, an average of 148 units per site. All cost figures are based on the month of May of 1985.

Very few support services are defined and standardized when a person enters congregate housing. The concept is not to provide a standardized level of service, but to introduce support at the margin at which individual residents need assistance with their own efforts to maintain an independent household. As a result, numerous cost assumptions are necessary.

Figure 1 summarizes the three levels of support service costs uncovered in the study. Based on previous assumptions, basic rent and utilities can be calculated including fair market rent equivalent of any rent subsidies.

FIGURE 1: Levels of Support Services in Congregate Housing

Level I: Baseline Congregate Support

These elderly people are the most independent and require only barrier-free and secure building design and congregate meals.

1. Basic shelter costs (rent plus utilities)
2. Full congregate meals cost (90 meals/month)
3. *Basic* sundry household budget
4. *Self-administered* laundry (8 loads per month)
5. *Public* transportation (32 one-way trips per month)

Level II: Intermediate Congregate Support

In addition to Level I services, these elderly people require some weekly assistance with housekeeping, and door-to-door transportation.

1. Basic shelter costs
2. Full congregate meals
3. *Basic* sundry household budget
4. *Self-administered* laundry
5. *Specialized* transportation — door-to-door service (16 one-way trips/month)
6. *Heavy* housekeeping (8 hours per month)

Level III: Advanced Congregate Support

In addition to Level I services, these elderly people require almost daily housekeeping assistance, some personal care, and one or more visits per week to monitor a health condition or provide minor medical assistance.

1. Basic shelter costs
2. Full congregate meals
3. *Advanced* sundry household budget
4. *Housekeeper administered* laundry
5. *Specialized* transportation — lift van (8 one-way trips per month)
6. *Heavy and light* housekeeping (16 hours per month)
7. Personal care (8 hours per month)
8. Nursing care (4 hours per month)
9. Any social recreation or counseling charges

Full congregate dining implies a standardization necessary to comparison with long-term care where all meals are included in facility charges. Each congregate facility required different amounts of group meals per month above the minimum of one per day for eligibility or study inclusion. How residents received the remaining meals was also extremely varied (personal shopping and cooking, restaurants, meals-on-wheels, additional meals purchased from the congregate housing kitchen, meals cooked by visiting housekeepers, eating with relatives, etc.).

As a result, a full 90 meals per month from the congregate housing kitchen was calculated, even though this typically *increased* the costs of congregate housing for most residents. The cost of dinner was directly expanded for 30 days to estimate the costs of noncongregate meals. Similarly, where the lighter meals are provided for weekdays, those costs can be expanded to the full 30 days. Where a facility does not provide the second or third meal, costs for such a meal were in proportion to the facility's dinner costs as derived from ratios of meal costs in facilities providing the other meals.

No extra costs are charged for special dietary meals. All seven congregate facilities report that they can provide special dietary modifications at no cost when the modification required is an adaptation of the regular meal being served (e.g., salt free, weighed portions for diabetics, pureed meats and vegetables, etc.). Residents requiring long-term special dietary modifications that cannot be similarly accommodated would be required to leave congregate housing (Diverticulitis is a common example of a long-term ailment mentioned by several congregate facilities that could not be accommodated in congregate housing).

Three sites used caterers, four sites used an on-site kitchen staff. Catered costs ranged from $174-$224 per person per room. The meals prepared on-site ranged from $209-$234.

Sundry living expenses is a cost totally overlooked in previous cost comparisons between long-term care and congregate housing. These are costs subsumed under the operating budget of long-term care facilities because they are under the control of the housekeeping staff and not the residents. The resident of a long-term care facility is not responsible for shopping for housekeeping provisions or for the upkeep of whatever private space and furniture they possess.

In congregate housing, the resident maintains an independent apartment and must provide all the sundry equipment and supplies needed for daily living. A budget for such supplies was calculated utilizing a sample household supply inventory and local market prices. These costs remain the same for Levels I and II residents. The average cost for all seven facilities was $19 per apartment per month. It assumes an initial supply of dishes, cooking utensils, cleaning equipment (e.g., a vacuum cleaner), flat linen, and medicine cabinet supplies. The $19 per month covers replacement and maintenance of these supplies. At Level III the average cost increases to $60 per apartment per month. This is based on the assumption that more specialized disposable items are required such as bed and chair pads and adult disposable diapers. Disposable paper products for incontinent residents are provided as part of the overall charge in the long-term care facilities in the study.

Transportation is another difficult cost to determine for congregate housing residents. The fact that they are still active in the larger community, and most are mobile, means that a great variety of both local and long distance trips are taken each month. Some housing managers feel that most trips are not vital to functional independence, are a matter of personal choice and life style, and should, therefore, be excluded from these cost calculations along with a number of other nonessential items that area matter of personal discretion. However, the majority of managers felt that the ability to venture out and control one's own shopping, banking, socializing, etc., was an essential characteristic of assisted independent living. This was considered so important that three of seven facilities owned or leased a van or limousine for the private use of facility residents.

Each level of congregate support requires a different type and amount of transportation. Level I residents, according to the managers, use conventional means of transportation and make the most trips. As summarized in Figure I, Levels II and III residents require more specialized transportation, but venture out less often according to the managers. As a result, average monthly costs actually decline from $10 to $6 to $3.

The housekeeping, personal care, visiting nurses, social and counseling services provided to congregate housing are primarily family, friends, and private agents hired by the resident or peripatetic community vendors. Where the management provides on-site services or contracts with a single outside provider on behalf of all the tenants, these charges to the residents are used. Where a wide variety of off-site providers are used at a facility, the primary community service provider is selected.

While community services are a logical common source of support, pricing their services requires another policy assumption. Most community services are nonprofit agencies subsidized by government grants and/or public contributions. Therefore they not only charge on a sliding scale, but charges are subsidized for all recipients. The study could derive costs by using either the charge to the resident for a service or the real cost to provide the service. In all cases *this study uses the charge to the resident* for the following reason. These services represent a community commitment to assist tax paying residents of the community. They are often not unique services to the elderly, and certainly not unique to congregate housing. A visiting public nurse, homemaker or transportation service is available to any community resident who can benefit from the service. Since the elderly residents of the community have paid into the tax system and contributed to community fund raising over a lifetime, they have, and are in effect, paying their fair share of the actual provider cost.

Before discussing the long-term care sample studied, it is important to understand what the three levels of support summarized in Figure 1 represent for the cost analysis. Congregate housing sites in the Midwest, and indeed nationally, are relatively new and still have relatively young and independent populations. Most of the sites are still below the average resident age and average level of resident assistance at which they will stabilize in years to come. As a result, the support profile of the average resident in the typical congregate facility today is likely to be Level I or II. However, to assume costs for congregate housing residents will remain at the lower levels is unrealistic and an unfair cost comparison.

In addition, in the course of conducting this study it was observed that despite their relative newness, several congregate facilities already had one or two residents who were more dependent than the Level III definition of advanced congregate support. However, in the course of evaluating the congregate facilities it became clear that the facilities could only accommodate the most severely frail and dependent elderly on a short term (3-6 months) or episodic basis, and then only a very small percentage of their total population could have such advanced and demanding dependencies. Therefore, it would be equally unrealistic to determine costs based on the most dependent elderly residing in congregate housing. Level III was established by identifying the most advanced level of support to which the *entire* population of congregate housing could evolve while still maintaining an assisted, independent living environment for all residents without changing the on-site support staff in size or character. In conclusion, these three levels represent distinct changes in the level of care and support services provided to residents, as observed in the congregate housing site interviews. However, none of the levels represent the true *norm* among congregate housing residents today. They were created to represent a fair cost range in cost comparisons with long-term care facilities.

Long-Term Care Sample

It was possible to focus entirely on Illinois long-term care facilities since there are 1072 state licensed facilities as of 1985. The universe from which the study sample was drawn was narrowed down to 330 facilities in order to make fair and accurate comparisons with the Congregate Housing sample. Along with restriction to urban areas described above, five variables define long-term care facilities as used in this study: type of licensing, type of ownership, building age, number of beds, and average facility cost per resident day.

In Illinois there are six basic types of licenses for long-term care facilities: skilled nursing care, intermediate nursing care, sheltered nursing care, intermediate care for the developmentally disabled, community long-term care, and child care (for persons under age 22). In addition, individual facilities may have combinations of skilled, intermediate and sheltered care licenses. Several licensing options were eliminated from the initial universe of long-term facilities for the purpose of this study. First, facilities licensed for child care and developmentally disabled care were eliminated for the obvious reason that they do not focus predominantly on the elderly. Second, facilities licensed exclusively for skilled care were eliminated. Skilled care is the most advanced stage of medical dependence and no residents at this stage can be transferred to congregate housing. Third, on the advice of the Illinois Department of Public Health, facilities that are exclusively licensed for sheltered care residents were also eliminated. By definition, sheltered care residents are the most functionally independent residents of long-term care facilities. However, currently in Illinois, facilities with this single licensure tend to house a disproportionate number of mentally disabled residents (elderly and nonelderly) with special care needs that are not duplicated in congregate housing. There are four combinations of skilled, intermediate and sheltered care licensed facilities that were included in the study universe: skilled, intermediate, and sheltered care; skilled and intermediate; intermediate and sheltered care; and intermediate care only. It was felt that facilities with these license combinations would house a large enough subset of residents with functional dependency characteristics similar to residents of congregate housing to warrant study.

Ownership type was also considered, using the same breakdown as congregate housing: (1) for profit, (2) not-for-profit, and (3) government facilities (e.g., county nursing homes). By crosstabulating the three ownership types and the four licensure types, a 12 celled matrix showing the proportion of sites to be sampled was attained. Unfortunately, the two largest cells were for profit skilled nursing and intermediate care facilities (44.5%) and for profit intermediate care facilities (26.1%). We ran into such a high rate of refusal to cooperate with these for profit facilities that we had to replace them with not-for-profit sites. However, the result when comparing ownership and licensure types on building age, size (number of beds), and average cost per resident day were very comparable. The final sites selected actually produced slightly lower costs per resident day then the for profit sites.

Average number of beds reflects facility size and economies of scale and efficiency in staffing, administrative and operating costs. The weighted mean score for the universe was 157 beds and the range of weighted means among license and ownership types was quite broad (95 to 285). Sampled sites were kept within this range.

Age of the facility instead of average age of the residents was used because long-term care facilities tend to be older and established institutions and the average age of residents is very similar across facilities. More important to the study of capital costs (discussed below) is that the buildings studied be near the mean age for the sample universe which was 1969. Average age of the facilities studied was between 1967 and 1975.

Average cost per person per day is the most direct way to be sure that a sample facility is not skewed toward one cost extreme or the other. Such a comparison was not possible with congregate housing in advance of site selection and analysis, but the Illinois Department of Public Aid does possess such data for long-term care facilities for 1982 (the most recent year). One sample site selected was within $3.50 of the weighted mean cost for all facilities in that ownership and license group. All the others were within $1.00 of the weighted group mean.

Once the long-term care sites were selected, a similar site visit and interview schedule was administered (June 1985), with one major exception. Field visits to the long-term care facilities in this study began after the congregate study site visits were completed and the three levels of congregate support were defined. It was already clear at that point that Level I residents were not included in most long-term care facilities. Because of the institutionalized nature of both service provision and cost accounting in long-term care facilities, it was *not* possible to separate costs at different levels of support similar to congregate housing. The respondents to the long-term care facility questionnaire were able to identify the number of residents that fit in the Level II-III support range, and were able to provide a single set of costs for the type and amount of services in this range.

There were a total of 1142 beds in the six facilities chosen with an average of 190 beds. A total of 536 (47%) of the long-term care residents in this study were deemed by management to be at a functional level that could be accommodated in congregate housing if it were available. However, the reader should not use this as a broad indicator because this study sought out long-term care facilities with high numbers of residents who were comparable to congregate housing residents, so that accurate cost comparisons could be made. In the remainder of this study the long-term care residents, who are functionally capable of congregate living, are referred to as "case study residents."

Daily Living and Support Costs
Excluded from the Study

Certain costs were not included in the study, either because field study found they were identical for both congregate housing and long-term care facilities or because no reliable norm could be established for the use and/or cost of the time or service. The types of costs excluded are:

1. Medical costs from a private physician, clinic or hospital. It is assumed that this is paid separately in both types of facilities and usually covered by Medicare, Medicaid, or private insurance.
2. Cost for prescription medicines, for reasons similar to those discussed for physician costs.
3. Clothing. For the same level of functional independence and activity, we assume similar clothing needs and costs in both congregate housing and long-term care facilities.
4. Out of town travel and private entertainment. These costs are quite variable from person to person, and no meaningful average can be calculated.
5. Nonessential sundry items. We assume residents of both facilities purchase candy, soft drinks, magazines, newspapers, etc. in equal amounts.
6. Hair care and podiatry. Costs for these services were collected in all site visits but were similar for residents of both congregate and long-term care facilities, and thus not included in this cost comparison.

Cost Comparison Using Existing Debt Services

Figure 2 shows the yearly savings with congregate housing using existing debt service to determine rent levels.

Income in long-term care facilities is limited to one fee per resident month. There are, however, two sources of income: private pay residents, where the rate and number of private pay residents is set by the facility, and public aid residents, where reimbursement rates are set by the state. The top half of Figure 2 uses the private pay rate. This is shown because the majority of case study residents (76%) are private pay. However, a more accurate and fair income per case study resident, would be to add private pay, and the much lower public aid, case study residents at each facility and derive an average actual income per case study resident used in the bottom half of Figure 2. The public aid rate by itself is not included, because this rate does not support the case study residents. Depending on the type of care license in each long-term care facility, public aid

FIGURE 2. Yearly Savings to Congregate Housing Using Existing Debt Service to Determine Rent Levels

	Charge Per Person Year	Savings Per Person Year[1]	Total Charges Per Facility Year[2] (in millions)	Savings Per Facility Year[1]
Private pay rate in long-term care facilities	$11,136		$1.65	
Congregate Housing charges:				
Level I	$ 7,980	$3,156	$1.18	$467,088
Level II	$ 8,172	$2,964	$1.21	$438,672
Level III	$ 9,192	$1,944	$1.36	$287,712
Long-term care facility charges with actual private pay/public aid mix	$ 9,492		$1.41	
Congregate Housing charges:				
Level I	$ 7,980	$1,512	$1.18	$223,776
Level II	$ 8,172	$1,320	$1.21	$195,360
Level III	$ 9,192	$ 300	$1.36	$ 44,400

[1]Savings are derived by subtracting congretage housing charges from long-term charges.

[2]Total facility charges are derived by multiplying per person charges for long-term care and congregate facilities by the average number of units (148) in the congregate facilities sampled.

residents are subsidized by private pay and/or public aid residents receiving a higher level of care.

The congregate housing costs are defined to represent private pay in so far as construction and management cost of the facility are concerned. There are several subsidies not shown such as low interest construction loans for some facilities and numerous community subsidies for visiting support services to individual residents. However, there are similar subsidies to long-term care facilities using the private pay rate. Most of these facilities are not-for-profit and receive property tax write offs and favorable construction loans.

The reader is also reminded that the researchers sought costs from both types of facility at all three levels of support. This was not possible given the management and billing procedures in long-term care facilities. As a result, Figure 2 compares a broad mean charge for all case study residents of the long-term care facilities studied, with three different levels of congregate support costs, none of which is truly representative of the average costs in congregate housing.

Cost comparisons using Level I support costs artificially favors congregate housing because this is the least expensive support cost level, yet the typical congregate facility will not retain a majority of residents at such a high level of functional independence over the life of the facility.

Cost comparisons using Level III congregate housing service costs artificially favors the long-term care facilities because, based on site observations, case study residents in long-term care are not concentrated at Level III. If all their case study residents were to reach Level III status, the typical long-term care facility would have much higher internal support costs and would most likely have to make financial adjustments by shifting some of the case study residents to a higher care level (and charge rate), and/or increase the ratio of private pay residents. The single best comparison would be the range of cost differences created by comparing Level II congregate housing charges with both private pay and private pay/public aid mixed charges for long-term care. This comparison produces a savings per person per year of $1320 to $2964 for residents of congregate housing. On a total facility basis, the savings per year range from $195,360 to $438,672 with congregate housing. However, two additional discussions are necessary to get a clear cost comparison; one is a refinement of the costs in Figure 2 normalizing capital costs and debt service. The second is re-examining the quality of life factors which cannot be priced.

Normalized Capital Costs and Debt Service

The savings shown in Figure 2 are considered a very conservative estimate because the congregate facilities tended to be built after 1980 and the long-term care facilities before 1970. This results in higher capital costs and debt service for congregate facilities. Normalizing capital costs and debt service to 1985 for all facilities results in a fairer comparison and simulates a cost for facilities being built and occupied in 1985.

Key to normalizing costs is the replacement value for the reporting facilities based on the most recent insurance underwriting assessments of the value of the building and its contents. When this figure is standardized per bed in long-term care facilities and per apartment, the per unit replacement value was almost identical among the sampled facilities ($41,691 and $39,401 respectively). The average congregate housing per unit replacement value of $39,401 is quite reasonable and cost competitive with conventional apartment construction; especially given that this replacement cost includes both a private apartment and a proportional share of congregate dining, social lounges, laundry room, and craft and recreation rooms. On the other hand, the $41,691 per bed figure for long-term care includes no totally private space and relatively little communal space unique to the case study residents. The per bed replacement cost does include communal space that must be divided among various care classifications, as well as space exclusive to the extensive on-site support and administrative staff. In the facilities that house skilled care residents, this per bed replacement cost also represents more stringent and costly building construction standards, furniture and equipment that is required by law in nursing care facilities.

To determine 1985 capital costs and debt service, a multiplier of 4.85 times the replacement value was derived from prevailing 1985 mortgage interest rates and a 25 year amortization period. It was then assumed all facilities could last 40 years without major alternations or replacements to the building. Total debt service was divided by 40 and by 12 to get monthly debt service per unit assuming no vacancy rate. The existing debt service on each facility is then subtracted from the 1985 normalized debt service. The difference in monthly debt service per unit or bed, is assumed to be the added expense if these facilities are to be built and begin operation in 1985. In order to maintain the profit margin or replacement revenue in each facility, this amount would also have to be added to the income side of the ledger and charged to each resident or apartment.

Figure 3 shows capital costs and debt service normalized to 1985. With the same arguments used in describing Figure 2, the fairest

FIGURE 3. Savings to Congregate Housing With All Capital Costs and Debt Service Normalized to 1985

	Charges Per Person Year	Savings Per Person Year[1]	Total Charges Per Facility Year[2] (in millions)	Savings Per Facility Year[1]
Private pay rate in long-term care facilities	$16,788		$2.49	
Congregate housing charges:				
Level I	$10,716	$6,072	$1.59	$900,000
Level II	$10,908	$5,880	$1.61	$880,000
Level III	$11,928	$4,860	$1.77	$720,000
Long-term care facility charges with actual private pay/public aid mix	$15,141		$2.24	
Congregate housing charges:				
Level I	$10,716	$4,425	$1.59	$650,000
Level II	$10,908	$4,233	$1.61	$630,000
Level III	$11,928	$3,213	$1.77	$470,000

[1]Savings are derived by subtracting congregate housing charges from long-term care charges.

[2]Total facility charges are derived by multiplying per person charges for long-term care and congregate facilities by the average number of units (148) in the congregate facilities sampled.

comparisons are with Level II congregate housing charges, or a savings range from $4233-$5880 if new congregate housing and long-term care facilities were built and began operation in 1985. For a facility with 148 apartments the savings of building and maintaining comparable elderly in congregate housing as opposed to a long-term care facility ranges from $630,000-$880,000 per facility year.

Quality of Life Factors

Perhaps the strongest criticism of congregate housing is that it relies heavily on community provided visiting services. Where these services are not present, present only on weekdays, not of high quality, or where need for such services is not carefully monitored and coordinated at the congregate facility, *undercaring* of residents can result. While this criticism may be valid in some facilities, it was not a major problem in the facilities sampled. This study was focused on urban areas with strong community peripatetic services. All the congregate facilities studied had staff trained to give counseling, information, and referral, and had a monitoring system to check on residents daily.

Criticism of the quality of life in long-term care facilities is far more extensive, especially when compared to the type of assisted independent living provided by congregate housing. Despite concerted efforts to identify and include the most progressive long-term care facilities in this study sample, all long-term care facilities limit the independence of residents when compared to congregate housing. At their worst, according to one study, they are custodial as opposed to rehabilitative environments that almost never provide or encourage independent living (Auston and Kasber, 1976). They often can encourage "learned helplessness" and docile dependence on support staff (Mercer and Kane, 1979). This can result in rapid atrophy of physical and social skills, making long-term care facilities a poor substitute for residents of similar support needs living in congregate housing.

The major differences were in the physical settings comparable case study residents received in congregate housing and long-term care. When comparing dining, the number of entree choices and choice of proportion sizes was very similar in both types of facility, as was the quality of food and menu ranges. The fact that all long-term care facilities separate skilled, intermediate and sheltered care residents in different areas of the facility, means that case study residents dine with others at their level of functional independence. Nevertheless, the congregate facilities tended to have dining rooms with less institutional appearance and provide more social flexibility and more casual atmosphere for dining. More guests were seen attending meals in the congregate facilities, and more congregate housing residents at all levels of support are away from the facility at mealtime.

The bottom line in physical cost comparisons is that despite the considerably higher costs the case study resident is getting much less in long-term care. He or she receives 100-150 square feet of semiprivate space around a bed in a nursing institution compared to 400-500 square feet of private apartment in congregate housing.

Unlike most long-term care facility residents, congregate housing residents retain control of their money, their personal affairs, their daily routine and the freedom to come and go as they please. Congregate housing appears to promote more self-sufficiency, encourage cost-saving interdependence with friends and neighbors in the facility and the community, offset social isolation and introduces costly professional support services only at the margin of individual needs.

CONCLUSIONS

The major reasons for the substantial costs savings with congregate housing are: (1) the elimination of expensive on-site personal and nursing care, and (2) the elimination of dependent living arrangements. Conversely, congregate housing is cost effective because it: (1) promotes independent living, (2) promotes self-sufficiency and/or interdependence with others in the private community (primarily congregate housing neighbors), (3) off-sets social isolation, and (4) brings in professional support only at the margin of individual need. The key to low cost congregate living for most elderly is the successful combination of a supportive physical environment, on-site social services, and personal capabilities employed to their fullest. For others it is just the small amount of regular visiting services that is the key to maintaining their independence.

The research staff was also impressed with the quality of care provided by the long-term care facilities studied. While the researchers strongly recommend that elderly with support needs that can be accommodated in congregate housing be provided congregate housing, this in no way implies that long-term care facilities do not provide excellent and important care for elderly with advanced frailties who *require* a dependent support environment. To the best of their abilities, all the long-term care facilities studied provided a homey atmosphere and caring and supportive staff. The fact remains, however, that it is almost impossible to provide both dependent and independent support environments under the same roof and by the same staff. The physical atmospheres and staff functions are in conflict. No matter how diligently the provider tries, a nursing institution is not and cannot serve as a private home. The level of state reimbursements to sheltered care residents as opposed to intermediate and skilled care residents is also in conflict. Sheltered care residents are reimbursed so much less, proportional to their support needs, that they become financially dependent on higher levels of care. This encourages either premature reclassification of sheltered care residents to higher care levels or lowering of sheltered care support quality.

REFERENCES

Anderson, E. "Report on the Congregate Housing Services Program," Public Housing Agency of the City of St. Paul, Minnesota, Unpublished Letter Report, April 1984.

Auston, M. and Kasberg, J. "Nursing Home Decision-Makers and the Social Service Needs of Residents." *Social Work in Health Care*, Vol. 1, 1976, pp. 447-56.

Booz, Allan and Hamilton. *Long-Term Care Study*. Volume II, State Department on Aging, Springfield, Illinois, 1975.

Butler, R. N. *Why Survive? Being Old in America*, New York: Harper and Row Publishers, 1975.

Canale, J. and Klinck, M. E. *Report of the Congregate Housing Study Committee*, Connecticut Department of Housing and Department on Aging, Hartford, April 1985.

Commonwealth of Massachusetts, *The 1984 Annual Report of the Executive Office of Elder Affairs*, The Commonwealth of Massachusetts, Boston, 1985.

Deetz, V. L. "Congregate Housing: A Growing Need." *HUD Challenge*, United States Department of Housing and Urban Development, Washington, DC, August 1979.

Gardner, A. *A Report on Maine's Congregate Housing Program*, Bureau on Maine's Elderly, Department of Human Services, Augusta, Maine, August 1984.

Heumann, L. F. *A Cost Comparison of Congregate Housing and Long-Term Care Facilities in the Midwest*, Illinois Housing Development Authority, Chicago, Illinois. September 1985.

Heumann, L. F. and Boldy, D. *Housing for the Elderly: Planning and Policy Formulation in Western Europe and North America*. New York: St. Martins Press, 1982, pp. 16-58.

Kistin, H. and Morris, R. "Alternatives to Institutional Care for the Elderly and Disabled." *Gerontologist*, Part I, Vol. 12, 1972, pp. 139-142.

Lawton, M. P. "Institution and Alternatives for Older People." *Health and Social Work*, Vol. 3, 1978, pp. 108-134.

Mercer, S. O. and Kane, R. A., 1979. "Helplessness and Hopelessness in the Institutionalized Aged: A Field Experiment." *Health and Social Work*, Vol. 4, pp. 90-116.

Molica, R. et al., *Congregate Housing for Older People: An Effective Alternative*. Final report. Massachusetts Department of Elder Affairs and Building Diagnostic, Inc., Boston, MA, June 1984.

Nachison, J. S. "Services for Congregate Housing: A New Direction for HUD." *HUD Challenge*, U. S. Department of Housing and Urban Development, Washington, DC, August 1979.

Nenno, M. K., Nachison, J. S., and Anderson, B. "Support Services for the Frail Elderly or Handicapped Persons Living in Government-Assisted Housing: A Public Policy Whose Time Has Come," working paper, February 1985.

New Jersey, Division on Aging, *Rules and Regulations: Congregate Housing Services Program*, Division on Aging, Congregate Housing Services Programs, April 1984.

Thompson, M. M. "The Elderly in our Environment: Yesterday and Today." *HUD Challenge*, United States Department of Housing and Urban Development, Washington, DC, August 1979.

Townsend, P. *The Last Refuge*, Routledge and Kegan Paul, London 1962.

United States House of Representatives, Select Committee on Aging, Subcommittee on Housing and Consumer Interests. *Congregate Housing Services*, U.S.G.P.O., Washington, DC, 1981, p. 47.

United States House of Representatives, Select Committee on Aging, Subcommittee on Housing and Long-Term Care. *New Perspectives on Health Care for Older Americans*. U.S.G.P.O., Washington, DC, January 1976.

Chapter 5

A Comparison of the Functional Status of Older Adults Living in Congregate and Independent Housing

Veronica F. Engle

SUMMARY. The functional status of congregate housing (Elderhouse) residents was evaluated and compared to older adults living in independent housing. Residents of both sites did not differ in their ability to perform everyday activities, as measured by the Sickness Impact Profile, but the older, better educated Elderhouse residents rated their health as better and had a slower walking pace. Results suggested that Elderhouse residents used mandatory services to maintain their level of function and independence, rather than to attain independence. The proposed resident of Elderhouse, the dysfunctional older adult, was not necessarily utilizing the semi-supportive environment. Additional factors, such as income, type of services and social image may be pertinent when designing and marketing semi-supportive environments.

With increasingly limited resources to meet the needs of an ever-expanding older population, health care providers and public planners are developing new services to prevent premature placement of

Veronica F. Engle, PhD, RN, is Associate Professor at the University of Tennessee, Memphis College of Nursing, 800 Madison Avenue, Memphis, TN 38163.

This study was supported by a grant from the Division of Nursing (HEW 5 R21 NU 00838-03).

The author wishes to thank D. Allen and B. Bowers for their review of this manuscript, and the residents and management of Elderhouse.

older adults in nursing homes. Questions arise, however, when designing and planning services concerning the needs of potential and/or actual users of services (Heller, Byerts, & Drehmer, 1984; Nasar & Farokpay, 1985). The opening of a new congregate housing facility, Elderhouse, provided the opportunity to evaluate residents' functional status or ability to performs everyday activities. This study was done in order to determine if Elderhouse residents had unique needs compared to older adults living independently in age-segregated, federally subsidized housing without such organized and planned services.

METHOD

Site

Elderhouse is a three-story remodeled motel located in the downtown area of a Midwest city with access to public transportation, retail stores, churches, health care services, and a library. Residents are free to come and go as they wish, and live in 62 one-room or 15 two-room apartments, with common living areas for meals and entertaining. All meals and housekeeping services are provided and a nursing clinic is available 20 hours a week. Provision of additional services, such as personal care, is co-ordinated by Elderhouse staff and obtained from public and private agencies. The entrance fee and monthly rent exclude older adults on limited incomes.

Sample

Twenty-three Elderhouse residents were interviewed sequentially as they moved into the new facility during its first 18 months of operation. The 17 (73.9%) women and 6 (26.1%) men, predominantly white, had a mean age of 81.2 years (SD = 10.3), and completed an average of 12.1 years of education (*SD* = 4.3). The majority (20) of participants were single, widowed, or divorced, with only three participants married.

The sample had a higher level of education than the general population of older adults. However, the city in which Elderhouse is located contains both the state capital and a major university. Thus, the community has many highly-educated older adults and this sample is representative of the community.

Instruments

Shanas Index of Disability

The Shanas Index of Disability (SID) (Shanas, Townsend, Wedderburn, Friis, Milhøj, & Stehouwer, 1968) was used to measure activities of daily living necessary for self-care. It contains six items each scored as independent (1) to dependent (3) on a 3-point scale. The SID measures a homogenous construct, discriminates between older adults living in the community and institutions, and evaluates less strenuous tasks necessary for independence (Chappell, 1981). It has been used primarily to evaluate older adults' functional ability in cross-national studies (Shanas et al., 1968).

Sickness Impact Profile

The Sickness Impact Profile (SIP) (Gilson, Bergner, Bobbitt, & Carter, 1978) was used to measure functional status by evaluating the impact of sickness on the ability to perform a wide variety of activities. These activities, as categorized by Lawton (1972), include perception-cognition, physical and instrumental self-maintenance, effectance and social role activities. Accordingly, the SIP measures a greater range of activity than usually found in functional status instruments for the aged.

The SIP has been validated on samples ranging in age from 18 to 81 years, with varying degrees of sickness. It was able to differentiate between different diseases as well as different degrees of severity of disease. The SIP differs from global self-assessments of health because items are concretely linked to participants' behavior (Snow & Crapo, 1982). The high level of reliability of the SIP is supported by test-retest coefficients and coefficients of internal consistency (Gilson, Bergner, Bobbitt, & Carter, 1978).

There are 136 items grouped into 12 categories, with points assigned each item relative to the degree of functional impairment due to sickness. (One category, "work," was omitted as all participants were retired.) The SIP is scored for overall activity, as well as physical and psychosocial dimensions of activity, with a higher score indicating greater impairment of function.

Self-Assessment of Health

Self-assessment of health (SAH) by older adults has been found to be a valid index of functional health (Engle & Graney, in press; Graney & Zimmerman, 1980), with satisfactory stability over repeated measurements of the same participants (Heyman & Jeffers, 1963). Wolinsky, Coe, Miller and Prendergast (1984) emphasized the importance of evaluating older adults' self-assessment of health as well as their ability to perform activities.

Self-assessment of health was measured using a modified Cantril Ladder (Engle, 1984) based on the technique originally proposed by Palmore and Luikart (1972). Participants viewed a 10-step ladder-like scale representing "your health today" with numbers one through ten appearing on consecutive steps. Calibrations included "lack of health" (rung 1), "average" (between rungs 5 and 6), and "perfect health" (rung 10).

Walking Pace

Walking pace (WP) was used to measure a qualitative dimension of functional status, speed (Engle, in press). Participants, wearing their customary footwear, walked in their natural or usual manner and were timed for 10 steps using a Heuer Trackmaster stopwatch. The test-retest coefficient of stability for walking pace was $r = .94$ (Engle, 1984).

Demographics

Age was recorded as the number of years old on the previous birthday and educational attainment as the number of years enrolled in formal schools.

Comparison Sample

The functional status, as measured by the SIP, SAH and WP, and demographics of the Elderhouse sample were compared to a simple random sample of 114 white older women living independently in age-segregated, federally subsidized housing complexes in a large Midwest city. The complexes did not offer planned, organized services. The comparison sample had a mean age of 76.4 years (*SD* = 7.2), and completed an average of 8.6 years of education (*SD* = 2.1). The majority of women were widows (78.9%), but 12.3% were divorced and 3.5% were married.

RESULTS

The frequency, mean, and standard deviation for each item of the Shanas Index of Disability are presented in Table 1. Table 2 presents the mean, standard deviation, and t-test for comparison of Elderhouse and independent housing residents' demographics and functional status (SIP-overall, SIP-physical, SIP-psychosocial, self-assessment of health, walking pace). A t-test for two independent samples was used, with an alpha level of .05 set as the criterion for rejection. Note that the separate variance estimate, as opposed to the usual pooled variance estimate, was used if the F-test for homogeneity of variance was significant, indicating unequal variance between the two samples. The separate variance estimate does not assume equal variance and is, therefore, more conservative (Nie, Hull, Jenkins, Steinbrenner, & Bent, 1975).

Results of the Shanas Index of Disability (see Table 1) demonstrated that Elderhouse residents Were relatively independent in moving about the house, washing/bathing, and dressing/putting on shoes, whereas the most difficult activities were cutting toenails and walking up and down stairs. These limitations in cutting toenails and using stairs, however, are typical for older adults in general (Shanas et al., 1968), and reflect physiological changes with age. Likewise, Elderhouse residents were fairly self-sufficient in their ability to perform a wide variety of everyday activities, as measured by the SIP, and did not differ from the independent housing residents on their ability to perform physical, psycho-social and overall activities. Note, however, that there were significant differences in self-assessment of health and walking pace, with Elderhouse residents rating their health as better despite a slower walking pace when compared to independent housing residents. Likewise, Elderhouse residents were significantly older and better educated.

TABLE 1. Results of Shanas Index of Disability for Elderhouse Residents[a]

Question	No Difficulty; No Assistance(1)	With Difficulty; No Assistance(2)	With Difficulty; With Assistance(3)	M	SD
1. Can you go outdoors?	16[b]	5	2	1.39	.66
2. Can you walk up and down stairs?	12	7	4	1.65	.78
3. Can you get about the house?	22	1	0	1.04	.21
4. Can you wash and bathe yourself?	18	3	2	1.30	.64
5. Can you dress and put on shoes?	20	3	0	1.13	.34
6. Can you cut your own toenails?	9	5	9	2.00	.91

[a] N = 23. [b] Frequency.

TABLE 2. Comparison of Elderhouse and Independent Housing Residents[a] Demographics and Functional Ability

	M	SD	t[b]
AGE			
Elderhouse	81.22	10.29	−2.12*
Independent	76.44	7.24	
EDUCATION			
Elderhouse	12.09	4.32	−3.79*
Independent	8.60	2.08	
SIP-OVERALL[c]			
Elderhouse	11.29	6.83	−.21
Independent	10.83	9.69	
SIP-PHYSICAL			
Elderhouse	11.32	8.82	−.76
Independent	9.72	9.23	
SIP-PSYCHOSOCIAL			
Elderhouse	7.23	6.97	1.33
Independent	9.64	11.38	
SELF-ASSESSMENT OF HEALTH			
Elderhouse	6.17	1.83	−2.01*
Independent	5.44	1.55	
WALKING PACE			
Elderhouse	73.32	30.60	5.78*
Independent	112.15	17.14	

[a] Elderhouse ($N = 23$); independent housing ($N = 114$). [b] Separate variance estimate used for age, education, walking pace and SIP-Psychosocial t-test. [c] SIP reported as percent score.

*$p < .05$.

DISCUSSION

The unexpected functional status of Elderhouse residents may have permitted them to utilize a semi-supportive environment which does not provide support for more basic, physical self-maintenance activities on a routine basis. Rather, support is provided in limited areas such as meal preparation and building maintenance. By providing such services, Elderhouse may have supported continued independence of residents who were no longer burdened with the day-to-day management of a household, rather than helping residents attain functional independence.

Regnier and Gelwicks (1981) found support for provision of limited services from the third of their sample of older adults with middle to high incomes who would even consider age-segregated housing as a viable living arrangement in the future. However, the overwhelming majority of respondents rejected mandatory support services such as meals or housekeeping, and preferred safety and security services first, followed by convenience services (such as grocery stores and pharmacies), health services (such as nursing clinics), and transportation. At Elderhouse, these preferred services as well as limited support services were provided to maintain a pre-existing level of function and lifestyle. The more intensive personal support services were appropriately contracted from public and private agencies as needed. Note, however, that the mandatory meals and housekeeping services may have actually been a marketing detriment rather than asset for potential Elderhouse residents (Varady, 1984). This may account for the length of time, more than 3 years, for Elderhouse to reach capacity.

The differences, rather than similarities, between residents in Elderhouse and independent housing may illustrate more clearly the characteristics of older adults choosing to live in a semi-supportive environment. Elderhouse residents were, on the average, almost 5 years older than residents in subsidized housing (see Table 2). They may have been breaking-up housekeeping for the first time due to a variety of reasons not necessarily related to decreased functioning. For example, the most common reason for moving into Elderhouse, inability to live alone, was cited by nine residents, but the next most frequent reason, to be near children, was cited by four residents. Four Elderhouse residents were also upset by the move and three preferred not to move. These numbers may reflect outside, unknown pressures to move into Elderhouse.

In contrast, the residents in independent housing had lived in their apartments for an average of 7 years, and may have broken-up housekeeping at an even earlier age than Elderhouse residents. This may have been due primarily to the availability of subsidized rent because the majority of independent housing residents were widowed females who typically experience a sharp drop in income with change in marital status. Elderhouse residents, on the other hand, may have had the financial ability to defer moving to a later date and to choose a more expensive rental unit when they did move. Consequently, there may be two distinct groups of older adults based on income rather than functional ability. Both groups may need semi-supportive services, but only more affluent older adults may be able to access these services.

Elderhouse residents also rated their health as better than independent housing residents (see Table 2). This may reflect better health and a higher level of functioning for their age, and may have permitted Elderhouse residents to delay their move into age-segregated and/or semi-supportive housing. Likewise, Elderhouse residents also may have needed a positive view of their own health in order to realistically assess their needs for maintaining independence, to be able to make such a decision, and to have a high enough level of function in order to move into and utilize Elderhouse and its services.

Last of all, the walking pace of Elderhouse residents was slower than independent housing residents (see Table 2). This slower pace may have increased both the time as well as energy needed to perform everyday activities. Thus, although the types of activities performed by Elderhouse and independent housing residents may have been similar, the quality of performance varied by speed (Engle, in press). This qualitative dimension of functional ability, speed, was reflected in a slower walking pace and may have been an additional factor in the decision to seek a semi-supportive environment.

A minimum level of function may, therefore, be necessary in order to make the decision to change environments. As older adults are more dependent upon environment cues (Muhlenkamp, Gress, & Flood, 1975) and a daily routine in order to maintain function, a move by a dysfunctional older adult, compared to a functional older adult, may be actually more debilitating. The dysfunctional older adult may not have the resources to deal with the new environment. The conventional wisdom of the positive benefits of moving into a semi-supportive environment may not always hold true. The requisite minimum level of function in order to cope with a new environment may help explain the equivocal results of previous relocation studies (Coffman, 1983).

Marketing can emphasize the maintenance of residents' independence and function, rather than their need for supportive services. Publicity should avoid depicting residents as dysfunctional, and describe residents as older adults who were able to make a graceful, yet desired transition to a living environment that eases demands for day-to-day maintenance of a house or apartment. This approach presents a positive social image, as compared to the negative image typically associated with a semi-supportive environment (Birenbaum, 1984). Proximity to convenience and health care services, with the freedom to leave the facility at will, could also be highlighted. As residents are more likely to be affluent, a middle- to upper-class lifestyle and values could be depicted.

However, the needs of the slower as well as older adult who may be utilizing a semi-supportive environment, as compared to independent housing residents, warrant close attention due to physiological changes with age and the corresponding impact on safety and architectural design. The potentially slower pace of the resident may require changes in design of the facility. For example, elevator doors and automatic entry/exit doors may need to remain open longer before closing, and the number of fire alarms and emergency exits may need to be increased as well as located closer to residents' bedrooms. Furniture in public areas may also need to be strategically placed in order to provide rest areas, and the building entrance should be close to parking as well as public transportation.

The older residents in Elderhouse ($M = 81.2$) may become dysfunctional and debilitated as they become older, yet live in an environment that may not change to meet their needs (Lawton, Moss, & Grimes, 1985). This changing rather than static functional status of residents could be addressed by administrative planning using an accommodating model to meet residents' changing needs with different types and amounts of support services. If the constant model is used, provision for the ongoing assessment of residents' functional ability and health, coupled with minimum criteria for function in order to remain in the facility, is necessary. On-site nursing services by skilled practitioners, such as geriatric nurse practitioners, can play an important role in the assessment of residents, the provision and/or coordination of support services, and the liaison with residents' families and friends. Inherent in this proposal, however, is the assumption that the aging process is variable and that residents' status may not all change at the same rate.

An important area for future study is identification of the parameters associated with the critical decision to change one's living situation, such as the type and number of persons participating in the decision-making process; the catalyst for change; the characteristics of available environments; the strengths needed for a successful decision and relocation; and, the individual's experience during the transition from one environment to another. This information may help prevent the all-too-familiar scenario of frail older adults who remain in the community and resist changing living environments until a crisis forces them into a nursing home. At that point, the older adult may be too incapacitated to function outside of a nursing home, and the decision to move to a supportive environment is made for, not by, the older adult. In contrast, Elderhouse residents sought services before debilitation, when they were able to participate in the decision-making process. Accordingly, health care providers and public planners should be cognizant that semi-supportive environments may not fill a unique need for dysfunctional older adults, but may provide a needed service for functional older adults that enables them to maintain their independence.

In summary, results of this study may indicate that the projected residents of Elderhouse, dysfunctional older adults, were not the actual residents of the semi-supportive environment. Elderhouse residents, when compared to independent housing residents, were older as well as slower but rated their health higher and performed the same number and types of activities. These differences, in addition to greater income, may have influenced their choice of Elderhouse and provide direction when designing and marketing semi-supportive environments.

REFERENCES

Birenbaum, A. (1984). Aging and housing: A note on how housing expresses social status. *Journal of Housing for the Elderly, 2*(1), 33-40.

Chappell, N. (1981). Measuring functional ability in chronic health conditions among the elderly. *Journal of Health and Social Behavior, 22*, 90-102.

Coffman, T. (1983). Toward an understanding of geriatric relocation. *Gerontologist, 23*, 453-459.

Engle, V. (1984). Newman's conceptual framework and the measurement of older adult's health. *Advances in Nursing Science, 7*, 24-36.

Engle, V. (1986). The relationship between older adults' functional health, movement and time. *Research in Nursing and Health*.

Engle, V., & Graney, M. (1986). Self-assessed and functional health of older women. *International Journal of Aging and Human Development*.

Gilson, B., Bergner, M., Bobbitt, R., & Carter, W. (1978). *The SIP: Final development and testing, 1975-1978*. Seattle: University of Washington, Department of Health and Community Medicine.

Graney, M., & Zimmerman, R. (1980). Health self-report correlates among older people in national random sample data. *Mid-American Review of Sociology, 5*, 47-59.

Heller, T., Byerts, T., & Drehmer, D. (1984). Impact of environment on social and activity behavior in public housing for the elderly. *Journal of Housing for the Elderly, 2*(2), 17-25.

Heyman, D., & Jeffers, F. (1963). Effect of time lapse inconsistency of self-health and medical evaluation of elderly persons. *Journal of Gerontology, 18*, 160-164.

Lawton, M. (1972). Assessing the competence of older people. In D. Kent, R. Kastenbaum, & S. Sherwood (Eds.), *Research planning and action for the elderly: The power and potential of social science*. New York: Behavioral Publications, Inc.

Lawton, M., Moss, M., & Grimes, M. (1985). The changing service needs of older tenants in planned housing. *Gerontologist, 25*(3), 258-264.

Muhlenkamp, A., Gres, L., & Flood, M. (1975). Perception of life change events by the elderly. *Nursing Research, 24*, 109-112.

Nasar, M., & Farokhpay, M. (1985). Assessment of activity priorities and design preferences of elderly residents in public housing: A case study. *Gerontologist, 25*(3), 215-257.

Nie, N., Hull, C., Jenkins, J., Steinbrenner, K., & Bent, D. (1975). *SPSS: Statistical package for the social sciences* (2nd ed.). New York: McGraw-Hill.

Palmore, E., & Luikart, C. (1972). Health and social factors related to life-satisfaction. *Journal of Health and Social Behavior, 13*, 68-80.

Regnier, V., & Gelwicks, L. (1981). Preferred supportive services for middle to higher income retirement housing. *Gerontologist, 21*(1), 54-58.

Shanas, F., Townsend, P., Wedderburn, D., Friis, H., Milhøj, P. and

Stenhouwer, J. *Old people in three industrial societies*. New York: Atherton Press: 1968.

Snow, R., & Crapo, L. (1982). Emotional bondedness, subjective well-being, and health in elderly medical patients. *Journal of Gerontology, 37*, 609-615.

Varady, D. (1984). Determinants of interest in senior citizen housing among the community resident elderly. *Gerontologist, 24*(4), 392-395.

Wolinsky, F., Coe, R., Miller, D., & Prendergast, J. (1984). Measurement of the global and functional dimensions of health status in the elderly. *Journal of Gerontology, 39*, 88-92.

Chapter 6

Which Elderly Home Owners Are Interested in Accessory Apartment Conversion and Home-Sharing

David P. Varady

SUMMARY. Previous researchers have found high levels of demand for, and utilization of housing programs by the better off elderly. This pattern of self-selectivity is *not* shown in the present article which examines the determinants of interest in accessory apartment conversion and homesharing among a sample of elderly homeowners in the Baltimore metropolitan area. Respondents who were under financial stress, as indicated by large uninsured medical expenses, and who were in poor health, were especially interested in these programs. The results indicate the importance of implementing accessory apartment conversion and homesharing in conjunction with counseling, low interest housing rehabilitation loans and other ancillary services.

INTRODUCTION

Accessory apartment conversion and homesharing are two nontraditional housing options which could help to maintain the independence of elderly homeowners. Accessory apartment conversion

Dr. David Varady, is Professor, School of Planning, University of Cincinnati, Cincinnati, OH 45221.

The author wishes to thank the Center on Aging, University of Maryland, for making available the data set on which this article is based.

involves the creation of a separate independent unit within an existing single family dwelling, with its own kitchen and bathroom. Typically, the basement is converted into a separate apartment although another section of the house is sometimes used. Accessory apartments are legal in only a small number of localities that have passed special zoning ordinances. The main advantage of an accessory apartment over homesharing, is the greater privacy; however it offers little flexibility to the owner who becomes dissatisfied with the apartment and wants to return to the original arrangement. In homesharing, the tenant or boarder may pay full rent or may barter his/her services in exchange for free, or a portion of room and possibly board. Local governments or social agencies play a role in matching homeowners seeking tenants, with individuals or couples seeking housing. Homesharing has the advantages of low cost and flexibility but offers less privacy than an accessory apartment.

Housing advocates have cited a number of individual and societal level benefits from these options including the additional rental income, companionship, help with housing repairs, and a better utilization of the housing stock. However, when these two programs have been made available, few elderly have taken advantage of them (Hare, 1985). Clearly, if homesharing and accessory apartment conversion are to become viable options for the elderly, program planners will require better information on the underlying causes of interest in them by the community resident elderly.

Up to now, there has been virtually no research on demand for these options among elderly homeowners. Most of what has been written on these options consists of either guidelines to owners on how to apply for and utilize the programs (e.g., American Association of Retired Persons, 1984) or descriptions of efforts to implement them (Gellen, 1985; Hamilton, 1987; Hare, n.d.; Pritchard, 1983). Of the few studies that have been conducted on the preferences of the elderly toward accessory apartment conversion, most have dealt with the experiences of elderly homeowners who have created accessory apartments (e.g., Hare and Guttman, 1984). Unfortunately, this research tells us little about the attitudes of community resident elderly without apartments.

We are aware of only two previous studies dealing with the attitudes of community resident elderly without apartments: Turner's

Housing Choices of Older Americans Project (Schreter and Turner, 1986; Turner and Mangum, 1982), and the author's 1985 study of accessory apartment conversion and homesharing in Montgomery County, Maryland. In the first phase of Turner's national study, 1,304 households were telephone interviewed for their demographic characteristics and to identify existing "sharers." In the follow-up mailed questionnaire returned by 38 percent of those interviewed, respondents were queried about their interest in homesharing and accessory apartment conversion. The 1986 article used bivariate crosstabular analysis to compare existing sharers, potential sharers, potential dividers and the total sample telephone interviewed.

This article improves on the Housing Choices study in four ways. First, our information on preferences and demographic characteristics was obtained from one data source, a telephone interview, thereby reducing bias. Second, our measure of interest in accessory apartment conversion is a more realistic one in that we do not, as in the earlier study, assume that the government will subsidize conversion costs. Third, we will use a multivariate statistical approach to assess the impact of different personal and housing characteristics on interest. This is a more appropriate approach for assessing the underlying causes of interest than a comparison of the characteristics of the interested and disinterested subgroups. Further, our use of a multivariate technique allows us to control for the interrelation among the independent variables whereas this was not possible in the Schreter and Turner article.

In the author's 1985 Montgomery County, Maryland study, 119 elderly homeowners were telephone interviewed to measure their interest in homesharing and accessory apartment conversion and to identify their reasons for interest/disinterest in the latter option. The study had three limitations. First, since the study's sample was drawn from a list of participants in the State's property tax credit program the research was skewed toward lower income elderly homeowners. Second, Montgomery County is not a typical suburban county. Income levels and housing costs are unusually high and the County is one of the few in the country to operate both a homesharing and an accessory apartment program. Consequently, levels of awareness and interest in these options may be unusually high.

Third, due to the wording of the question measuring interest, it is impossible to determine how much overlap exists in preferences toward the two options. That is, respondents were asked which option they preferred most; the results mask respondents who are interested in both. This article builds upon the Montgomery County research by using a sample with a wider range of incomes; by surveying a more typical urban and suburban area and by using two separate questions to measure interest in homesharing/accessory apartment conversion.

This article seeks to add to the limited social science literature on the ability of housing programs and social services to reach the elderly in greatest need. Lawton (1980) notes that senior citizen housing often does not reach those in greatest need for two reasons. The first, administrative discretion, the tendency to select less needy tenants, has received some attention in the literature, but the other, self-selectivity, has received virtually none. Research on social services indicates that the least needy are most likely to generate the demand for particular services (Kahana et al., 1976). One would expect the same pattern of self-selectivity to exist for accessory apartment conversion and homesharing. That is, the "young-old" as well as highly educated and affluent elderly would be most interested in these options because they would possess the capacity to make whatever housing modifications were necessary and would be more capable of overseeing tenants. This article seeks to determine whether these same patterns of self-selectivity from among the least needy do, in fact, exist for homesharing and accessory apartment conversion.

METHODS

This paper is based on a telephone survey of 171 elderly householders (ranging in age from 59 to over 85 years old), conducted for a church denomination in the Baltimore metropolitan area. Householders were first sent a letter from the Church requesting their participation; individuals were asked to indicate their willingness to participate in the study by filling out an application and returning it to the researchers.

One hundred seventy one interviews were completed out of the

225 applications returned. Our analysis in this paper is limited to the 132 completed interviews with homeowners, approximately four fifths of the sample.[1]

The survey covered attitudes toward different housing options (accessory apartments, homesharing, senior citizen housing), health and functional ability, as well as other background personal and housing characteristics.

In order to measure interest in accessory apartments, homeowners were asked:

> Would you be interested in creating an apartment with a separate entrance within your current home? (No/Yes/Maybe)

Later in the survey, respondents were asked:

> Would you be interested in a service that matches up potential renters with homeowners who would like to rent a room or apartment? (No/Yes/Maybe)

Only about a tenth (14 percent) of the owners were interested in homesharing and even a smaller proportion (9 percent) were interested in accessory apartment conversion. This does not mean that 23 percent of the sample were interested in one or both options since respondents could express interest in both options, resulting in double counting. In order to more accurately determine the number interested in one or both options, we crosstabulated the two preference questions. Of the 24 or 18 percent of the total who were so interested, 6 were interested in both strategies, 6 were interested in accessory apartments only while the remaining 12 preferred homesharing.

Stepwise discriminant analysis is used to test for the relative importance of different personal, housing and neighborhood characteristics in distinguishing those householders interested and not interested in accessory apartment conversion/homesharing. The stepwise discriminant procedure chooses the single best discriminating variable and then pairs the initial variable with each of the other independent variables one at a time to increase the discriminating power of the function. Variables not contributing significantly toward further classification are excluded. Table 1 presents

Table 1. Discriminant analysis results, factors distinguishing between elderly householders not interested and interested in accessory apartment conversion/ homesharing. Standardized discriminant coefficients.

Characteristic	Accessory apartment conversion	Homesharing
Demographic indicators of need and capacity		
Income	a	-.35
Uninsured medical expenses	.80	.29
Financial assets for emergencies	a	a
Educational level	a	-.29
Neither spouse works	.23	a
Age of respondent	-.35	a
Live alone	.29	a
Female	a	a
Black	a	a
Health		
Physical health fair to poor	.36	a
Difficulty climbing stairs	a	.60
Neighborhood attachments		
Length of residence at location	a	.56
Considering moving	a	.28
Housing/neighborhood characteristics		
Detached home	a	a
House value	.31	.43
Own home free and clear	-.48	-.36
Wilk's lamda	.6864	.7400
Chi-square	36.683	28.783
N	101	101
Significance	.0000	.0003
Eigenvalue	.4568	.3455
Percent of grouped cases correctly classified	86.8%	78.07%

the findings for all of the variables hypothesized to be important including those not in the final discriminant functions.

Table 1 shows that the discriminant function performed well correctly classifying nearly nine tenths (87 percent) of the cases with respect to accessory apartment conversion and nearly four fifths (78 percent) with respect to homesharing. Moreover, the results are revealing in terms of the underlying causes of interest in these options.

FINDINGS

Demographic Indicators of Need and Capacity

A priori, it was difficult to anticipate what impact the householder's financial status would have on his/her interest in accessory apartments and homesharing. On the one hand, the more financially strapped householders might be attracted to these options because of the additional rental income. On the other hand, relatively affluent elderly owners might be especially interested in having an accessory apartment because they would be better able to afford the home modification.

Table 1 supports the "need" hypothesis over the "capacity" one. Large uninsured medical expenses was one of the most important predictors of interest in both homesharing and accessory apartment conversion. In addition, low incomes promoted interest in homesharing while employment status (i.e., the fact that neither spouse worked) sparked demand for accessory apartment conversion.

We expected education to have more of an impact on interest in homesharing than on interest in accessory apartment conversion. Historically, working class families have taken in boarders in later life in order to obtain additional income (Gellen, 1985). This implies that within our sample, those with a high school degree or less would be more likely to be interested in this option than those with a college education. Table 1 supports this assertion; formal education is negatively correlated with interest in homesharing.

In contrast, we anticipated that education would be positively correlated with interest in accessory apartment conversion. That is, the more highly educated elderly would be more likely to be aware of this non-traditional housing option from information in newspapers, magazines, etc. Furthermore, formal education would contribute to a greater willingness to deal with government agencies in applying for participation. In reality, formal education had no significant impact with respect to accessory apartment conversion.

We expected that accessory apartment conversion and homesharing would be especially attractive options for the elderly living alone since having someone else under the same roof would alleviate feelings of loneliness. Living alone did have the expected impact, but for accessory apartment conversion only. It is not apparent why this option did not affect interest in homesharing.

Within the single elderly population, we expected women to be more interested in homesharing than men but we did not expect sex to be a significant determinant in the case of accessory apartment conversion. Historically, homesharing has involved widows taking in boarders in order to make ends meet. The "caring" roles that women perform earlier in their lives prepare them better for running a house and for sharing housing space. In contrast, men may be more capable of creating accessory apartments. Their pre-retirement jobs, as well as their roles within the family, prepare them better for working with contractors, banks and government agencies in making home modifications. As shown in Table 1, neither of these hypotheses dealing with the sex of the respondent was supported.

It was assumed that age would be negatively correlated with interest. Although many "old-old" respondents might benefit from having a boarder or from having an accessory apartment, few would have the financial, emotional or physical capacity to carry out these two options. Table 1 supports this assertion for accessory apartment conversion only.

On the basis of previous research we expected blacks to be more interested than whites in homesharing and accessory apartments. The black elderly have stronger kinship ties than their white counterparts (Chatters et al., 1986) and it is not uncommon for the black elderly to live in the same dwelling as their children and grandchildren. Although it seemed reasonable to assume that intergenerational living leads to a greater willingness to share housing space, this hypothesis was not supported by the discriminant analysis.

Health

We assumed that only those who were healthy would be capable and willing to go through what might be perceived of as an arduous process of supervising a conversion and/or selecting a tenant for a homesharing arrangement. Table 1 shows just the opposite to be true. That is, those in poor health were more likely to be interested in accessory apartments while those with limited functional ability (i.e., who had difficulty in climbing stairs) were more likely to be interested in homesharing. Many of those who were interested may have been recovering from severe health problems (Schreter, 1983) and may have been attracted to homesharing/accessory apartment conversion by the additional rental income or the assistance with chores or home repairs that a tenant could provide.

Neighborhood Attachments

It was assumed that those who lived at their locations longest would have the strongest social ties there. Such householders would be concerned about the adverse reactions from neighbors to taking in boarders or to creating an accessory apartment, and therefore would be less likely to be interested in the two strategies. Surprisingly, long term residence was correlated with interest, not disinterest.

We were even more certain that interest would be negatively correlated with moving plans since households with relocation intentions would be unlikely to invest the time or money in rearranging their house or in finding a tenant. The fact that those with plans to move were more likely to be interested in homesharing therefore comes as a surprise (Table 1). Perhaps the moving plans variable served as an indicator of community attachment rather than as a predictor of when the family would move. That is, families with relocation plans and who were weakly integrated into the surrounding community might have been less concerned about neighbors' reactions to taking in a boarder, thereby making them more likely to be interested. Additional research is warranted to explain this surprising finding.

Housing and Neighborhood Characteristics

We assumed that homeowners with excess housing space would be especially interested in accessory apartment conversion or homesharing. Unfortunately, the survey did not include any direct objective or subjective measures of space adequacy. Two proxies were available, however: housing type (attached or detached) and housing value. We assumed that those living in relatively expensive, detached homes would be more likely to be "overhoused" and as a result would be more likely to be interested in accessory apartments and homesharing. Table 1 shows that as predicted, housing value was one of the most important predictors of interest in both options. However, housetype did not play a significant discriminatory role.

Earlier we found that families experiencing financial stress (as indicated by low incomes, large uninsured medical expenses, etc.) were more likely to be interested in these two non-traditional housing options. This implies that householders who had not paid off their mortgage would be interested in homesharing and accessory apartment conversion in order to cope with high housing costs. Table 1 supports this assertion for both homesharing and accessory apartment conversion.

Civic associations in suburban communities have frequently opposed the implementation of homesharing and accessory apartment programs, reflecting the widely held belief that these options undermine the family character of these newer areas. We assumed that when all other factors were controlled, those seeing themselves in "urban" type neighborhoods (i.e., with higher density levels, older homes) would be more interested in accessory apartment conversion or homesharing because they would feel that these non-traditional housing arrangements would be compatible with their urban location. In fact, the locational context, (urban or suburban), played no significant role in the discriminant analysis.

CONCLUSIONS AND POLICY IMPLICATIONS

This article is one of the first to examine the underlying causes of elderly homeowner interest in accessory apartment conversion and homesharing. Multiple discriminant analysis was applied to a telephone interview sample of 132 elderly homeowners in the Baltimore, Maryland area to determine the relative importance of different personal, housing and neighborhood characteristics in affecting interest.

The results highlight need as a cause of interest in both options rather than the capacity to carry out the conversion or manage a homesharing arrangement. That is, low income, large uninsured medical expenses, poor health, and an inability to climb stairs were important predictors of interest. Furthermore, there was strong indirect evidence that homeowners sought these two programs in order to use their housing space more efficiently. Those living in the more expensive detached homes, which undoubtedly were the larger ones, were more likely to be interested than those living in cheaper homes or attached ones.

There were several key differences in the determinants of interest between homesharing and accessory apartment conversion. Two factors influenced interest in accessory apartment conversion only: age (negatively), and living alone. Three other factors affected demand for homesharing but not accessory apartment conversion: educational level (negatively), length of residence and moving plans.

Our results differ from those obtained in earlier research which indicated higher levels of demand for/utilization of housing programs and social services by the "better off" elderly. In this study, many of the elderly subgroups at risk in terms of premature institutionalization (e.g., those living alone, those in poor health) expressed the highest levels of interest in these two programs. Self-selectivity may be less of a problem than some scholars have suggested.

This latter conclusion poses a difficult challenge for policymakers. Those interested in homesharing and accessory apartment conversion often lack the physical, emotional and financial capacity to find a tenant or to create an accessory apartment. Counseling, low interest housing rehabilitation loans and other ancillary services will have to be provided in conjunction with homesharing/accessory apartment conversion in order to insure that those who are interested actually participate in these programs.

NOTE

1. Since this study is based on a sample from one church denomination in one metropolitan area, it is not intended to be a representative sample of the elderly. Nevertheless, there were surprisingly small differences between the elderly in the sample and the elderly nationally with respect to the proportions of owners (78 percent versus 72 percent). The sample reported on here is, however, more affluent and better housed than the national elderly population. Both the median income and median housing values in the sample were twice as large for the sample ($22,846 versus $8,904 for income and $76,667 versus $38,900 for housing value). Appendix Table 1 provides additional descriptive information on the sample interviewed.

This predominantly suburban (75 percent) sample should be valuable for policymaking. Housing advocates have seen accessory apartments and homesharing as particularly useful for middle income suburban elderly owners but up to now there has been inadequate information available on interest levels in this group.

Data on the national elderly population are drawn from U.S. Congress, 1985. Even though there were respondents in the sample as young as 59, only the data for those 65 and over is used in order to insure comparability with the national results. It should be noted that the discriminant analysis utilizes the full sample of elderly owners telephone interviewed.

REFERENCES

American Association of Retired Persons. With the Federal Trade Commission. 1984. Your Home, Your Choice: A Workbook for Older People and Their Families. Washington, D.C.:AARP and FTC.

Chatters, L.M.; Taylor, R.J.; and Jackson, J.S. 1986. "Aged Blacks' Choices for an Informer Helper Network." Journal of Gerontology, 41, 1 (January), 94-100.

Gellen, M. 1985. Accessory Apartments in Single-Family Housing. New Brunswick, N.J.: Center for Urban Policy Research.

Hamilton R. 1985. "Helping the Elderly Keep their Homes." New York Times. January 4, 1987.

Hare, P.H. n.d. Using Surplus Space in Single-Family Houses. Planning Advisory Service, Number 365. Chicago: American Planning Association.

Hare, P.H. and Guttman, D. 1984. Accessory Apartments: A New Housing Option for the Elderly Homeowner. Report to the AARP-Andrus Foundation. Washington, D.C.:Catholic University.

Kahana, E.; Felton, B.; and Fairchild, T. 1976. "Community Services and Facilities Planning." In Community Planning for an Aging Society. (eds. M. Powell Lawton et al.,) Stroudsburg, Pa.: Dowden, Hutchinson and Ross.

Lawton, M.P. 1980. Social and Medical Services in Housing for the Aged. Washington, D.C.:National Institute of Mental Health.

Pritchard, D.C. 1983. "The Art of Matchmaking : A Case Study of Shared Housing." The Gerontologist. 23, 2.

Schreter, C.A. and Turner, L.A. 1986. "Sharing and Subdividing Private Market Housing." The Gerontologist. 26, 2 (April), 181-186.

Turner, L.A. and Mangum, E. 1982. Report on the Housing Choices of Older Americans: Summary of Survey Findings and Recommendations for Practitioners. Washington, D.C.: National Council on Aging.

U.S. Congress. Office of Technology Assessment. 1985. Technology and Aging in America. Washington D.C.: Government Printing Office.

Varady, David P. 1985. Accessory Apartment Conversion in Montgomery County, Maryland. Cincinnati: School of Planning, University of Cincinnati.

Appendix Table 1. Demographic characteristics of study sample. Owners 65 and above, N=98.

Characteristic	Proportion
Neighborhood type	
Central city	21%
Suburb	75
Rural	4
Housing type	
Single detached	78%
Apartment	4
Rowhouse	18
Race	
White	92%
Black	7
Other	1
Sex	
Male	31%
Female	69
Marital status	
Never married	4%
Married	59
Widowed	34
Divorced	2
Separated	1
Age	
65-69 years	31%
70-79 years	57
80 yrs. and older	12
Education	
High school degree or less	33%
Some college	28
B.A. degree or above	39
Family income	
Below $4,000	2%
$4,000-$7,999	5
$8,000-$11,999	12
$12,000-$17,999	17
$18,000-$23,999	15
$24,000 and above	49

Chapter 7

Senior Resident vs. Senior Highrise – Liability for Transferring Elderly Residents

Leonard H. Hellman

SUMMARY. The underlying issue facing our society with a growing elderly population is to be able to provide a continuum of care which would allow suitable and smooth movement along a spectrum of health and housing services. Many frail elderly are faced with an "all or nothing" approach to their housing needs; that is, being placed in a nursing home when they can no longer live independently. Alternatives to nursing homes include adult day care, senior health centers, meal programs and assisted living centers. In the U.S. many of these alternatives are only recently evolving. In the meantime a case managed approach which objectively evaluates and updates a frail resident's functional level and helps determine when it is time to move and assures communication among the parties, is sorely needed.

In a recent case a local highrise was sued for transferring a 90 year old woman from her apartment to a nursing home. The City Department of Social Services was joined in the suit. Plaintiff's attorney alleged that neither the highrise staff nor the Department of Social Services provided the resident or her family with adequate communication regarding the transfer and violated her civil rights in moving her to a nursing home. The jury, in awarding the Plaintiff a sizeable sum, gave a clear message that such an action by the hous-

Leonard H. Hellman, MD, LLB, is President, Colorado Gerontological Society, and Medical Director, Mercy Senior Health Center, 3202 West Colfax Avenue, Denver, CO 80204.

ing staff, in cooperation with the Department of Social Services, was serious business and required appropriate communication, a high level of sensitivity and adequate protection of the resident's due process rights.

As more and more seniors seek housing accommodations in senior highrises, congregate living centers and assisted living settings, it will become incumbent upon the housing staff which may include social workers and case managers to establish clearly defined criteria for transferring an elderly resident out of their apartment or home and into a more structured and supportive environment such as a nursing home. As decisions regarding housing placement become more difficult, baseline data, objective risk analysis and a formal process of assessment, review, communication and appeals will be needed to protect the rights of senior citizens. The extreme cases in which an elderly resident becomes severely confused or unable to care for himself/herself are not in issue, for in these instances there is general agreement among the parties that a more supportive environment is necessary. In most cases however, chronic disease, whether it be confusion due to dementia, incontinence or Parkinson's, progress in an insidious manner.

At what point should a senior be transferred is a difficult and critical determination. Many seniors view themselves as younger and more vigorous and independent than their years and function belie. To quote Bernard Barush, "Old age is always 15 years older than I am." Many residents also have an inordinate fear of being placed in a nursing home. It becomes evident that a growing number of elderly residents will either deny their ailments or refuse to voluntarily leave their apartments for a more supportive or protective environment. Their family members will also be reluctant to see their mother or father transferred against their will to a nursing home.

It is also important to protect the actions of the housing staff who act in good faith in transferring elderly residents who can no longer maintain themselves with an adequate level of independence in their present environment and who pose a danger to themselves and other residents. A person may enter a senior highrise or a personal care boarding home in relatively good health, however, in due course many will deteriorate from exacerbation or progression of chronic disease or from an acute process such as a stroke.

There are often no clear cut answers as to whether a patient or resident can maintain himself/herself safely and independently in a senior highrise and much depends upon the subjective judgement of staff, family, patients and physician. Many times these views differ. These are the cases that require an objective and well defined process for determining an elderly resident's ability to keep their present abode or be transferred, even involuntarily, to a more restrictive environment.

Involuntarily removing a senior from his/her apartment can lead to increased liability of this specialized segment of the housing industry unless an effective process is employed to assure due process and protection of a resident's rights. Transfers of this nature are a traumatic experience often referred to in the gerontologic literature as "transfer trauma." Most senior housing facilities merely require that the resident be independent and able to maintain himself/herself in their apartment. The question as to whom makes this determination and under what circumstances is often ill defined and the basic desires of the resident and family may conflict with the interests of the highrise staff. Poorly defined criteria which leave these important determinations to a single social worker whose case load is often too large for personalized care, are subject to abuse and open the highrise to legal action. It was fascinating to watch the attorneys argue their points regarding just how much incontinence actually existed and what level of incontinence would justify a transfer. Obviously it would be preferable to have the social worker, physician and family constructively discuss the issue of incontinence rather than the legal profession in an adversarial environment.

Is urinary incontinence or increasing confusion enough to warrant a transfer? What level of confusion is unacceptable and to what point is the resident a danger to himself/herself or other residents? Is it merely more expedient and financially acceptable to transfer a senior out of a highrise so that their apartment can be made available to a younger and more independent person?

Not only must the housing facility establish clearly defined criteria for transfer they must also implement ongoing assessment of all residents by trained and sensitive staff. In short, a formalized process ·is needed. One obvious approach is to develop a computerized case-management assessment of each resident which results in an objective baseline evaluation upon entering their domicile.

Social workers or case managers can utilize the baseline assessment made upon admission to determine the level and significance of functional change (see following example). Periodic updates are mandatory and will raise a red flag prompting further evaluation of residents in need of assistance in a timely and effective manner. This approach will help assure prompt intervention to maximize independence. A formal system of review of each resident at risk of transfer as well as an appeals process should also be implemented. Appropriate communication with the resident and family members is also mandatory (documentation is critical). Case management criteria are being developed by a number of health and housing programs. These criteria usually identify and rate variables including ability to dress, bathe, shop and cook, include assessment of bowel and urinary function as well as mental status. Each criteria is weighted in relation to their effect on activities of daily living (ADL) and level of independence, so that bowel incontinence might in and of itself produce a risk score that could support transfer out of the housing unit.

An objective evaluation will hopefully result in a numerical score which reflects the resident's true level of independence and will assist highrise professional staff as well as physicians, family and senior residents to understand functional disabilities and provide a more acceptable basis for transfer. The rating would be similar to the APGAR score for new-borns or to scores in mental status evaluations. Ideally, such a system would be accepted on a national or regional basis thus providing an objective and accepted method for supporting transfers. Each housing facility could customize the scoring as well as the criteria and assessment process. It will be impossible and inappropriate to avoid a totally subjective determination as to when it is appropriate to transfer someone to a nursing home and it must be understood that the acuity scores are guidelines to assessing a resident's functional capacity.

EXAMPLE OF COMPUTERIZED WELLNESS PROFILE:

FUNCTIONAL ASSESSMENT

Resident Name: SMITH, SALLY   Resident ID #0000001
Functional Assessment Scores: 0 = least independent; 5 = most independent

Assessment Dates:	04/25/87	08/26/87	01/11/88	02/09/88
Apartment Maintenance	4	4	4	3
Bathing	4	4	4	4
Expressive Communica	4	4	5	5
Receptive Communica	5	4	4	4
Continence (urinary):	5	4	4	2
Emotional Status	4	4	4	3
Grooming & Dressing	5	4	4	3
Hearing	5	5	5	5
Meal Preparation	5	4	3	2
Medications	5	4	4	3
Mobility	4	4	4	4
Money Management	5	4	3	3
Orientation	5	5	4	4
Physical Health	5	4	4	3
Shopping	5	4	4	3
Social Activities	5	5	3	3
Support Network	4	5	4	4
Toileting	5	5	4	3
Travel	4	4	4	2
Vision	4	4	4	3
ACCUITY	**4.6**	**4.25**	**3.6**	**3.3**

RECOMMENDATION:
Independent -   4.25 & 4.6   Action Plan:
Assisted Living -   3.6 & 3.3
Nursing Home -   Not Applicable

Chapter 8

Influence of Income on Energy Beliefs and Behaviors of Urban Elderly

Colleen K. Mileham
Jeanette A. Brandt

SUMMARY. Although public attention toward residential energy costs has diminished in the past few years, meeting energy costs remains a concern for the elderly population. The impact of income on energy beliefs and behaviors of urban elderly indicate that lower income elderly may be adversely affected by residential energy costs. The results of this study indicate that urban elderly with lower incomes engage in more lifestyle cutbacks and curtailment behaviors than do those with higher incomes. This research emphasizes the need to investigate energy policies that target low income elderly.

Public concern over residential energy costs has diminished over the past few years and many Americans no longer view energy as an urgent national issue (Anderson et al., 1987; Coltrane, Archer & Aronson, 1986; Savitz, 1984). The decrease in oil prices, due to a reported oversupply, makes the energy crisis seem like a thing of

Colleen K. Mileham, MS, is a doctoral student and Jeanette A. Brandt, PhD, is Associate Professor in Family Resource Management, College of Home Economics, Oregon State University, Corvallis, OR 97331.

Mail correspondence to: Colleen K. Mileham, College of Home Economics, Oregon State University, Corvallis, OR 97331.

Data and analysis for this study were provided by the Western Regional Agricultural Experiment Station Project (W-159): "Consequences of Energy Conservation Policies for Western Region Households," which was partly funded by a grant from the U.S. Department of Agriculture. Oregon Agricultural Experiment Station Technical paper number 8424.

107

the past. Nevertheless, given the importance of energy conservation in the last decade, an existing attitude prevails that energy conservation must continue (Brown & Rollinson, 1985; Gibbons & Chandler, 1981; Hirst, 1985).

Concern over the energy problems of the elderly has been the focus of much discussion and research since the outset of the energy crisis over ten years ago. The vulnerability of the elderly to increasing energy costs has been attributed to the impact of such factors as the aging process on health and body functioning (Pepmiller, 1981; U.S. Senate Committee on Aging, 1982), the age of dwelling units (Cooper, 1981; White, 1985), and the income status of many elderly. Although the literature indicates that the elderly as a group have fared better economically than other groups (Longman, 1985; Pitts, 1986), they also spend a greater proportion of their income on energy consumption, 14.1% of the elderly live in poverty and 22.4% are among the "near poor"—i.e., those whose incomes fall below 125% of the poverty level (Cook & Kramek, 1986). Therefore, what impact do energy costs have on various income levels of the elderly?

BACKGROUND

Previous research has supported the contention that the elderly population's life cycle stage and income level provide a unique set of circumstances which determine energy consumption and expenditure (Morrison & Gladhart, 1976; Warriner, 1981). Newman and Day (1975) indicated that the poor and elderly consume less energy than other income and age groups due to changes in lifestyle. Brown and Rollinson (1985) also found energy consumption to increase through the child raising years, but to decline after children left the household.

Although energy consumption appeared to decline with age, the elderly still paid proportionally more for energy in relation to income than the average residential customer (Cooper, 1981). Marganus and Badenhop (1984) did not find a significant difference in the energy budget of age groups under 65 years of age but found that individuals of retirement age spent twice as much of their incomes on energy costs. Katz and Morgan (1983) found that elderly were not as economically secure and spent a higher portion of their income on energy. Kennedy (1980) contended that the low income elderly are burdened less than other low income populations because consumption is less; however, dwellings are smaller and household size has decreased; but the burden still remains great for the elderly population.

A variety of studies have suggested why elderly spend a larger proportion of their incomes on energy and therefore appear to be less energy conserving. Much of the energy used by this population is based on health and comfort. Pepmiller (1981) discussed the impact of reduced temperature in buildings and homes resulting in hypothermia for many elderly. Fluctuations in temperature can be a major threat to many elderly due to health problems and decreased activity. Pepmiller recommended that homes and public buildings be as warm as possible to accommodate physical needs of this population. Royce and Iams (1982) also concluded that adequate use of energy resources to maintain well-being of the elderly population was of greater importance than energy conservation.

Further evidence of higher energy expenditures by the elderly relate to the size and age of many of their dwellings. White (1985) indicated that half of elderly housing was built before World War II and lacked energy efficiency. Many of the homes were deficient in conservation measures which required capital investments, especially insulation and storm windows (Brown & Rollinson, 1985). Elderly were also found to be less handy at home improvements and repairs, thus imposing additional costs of having others implement conservation measures. Although conservation measures are costly for elderly, tenure appears to have a great impact on improving energy efficiency of a dwelling concomitantly with a propensity to engage in conservation practices.

Marganus (1984) found the size of a dwelling was the best predictor of money spent on energy, with over 21 percent of the variance in energy costs attributed to the size of the dwelling. Morrison et al., (1978) concurred, finding that the number of rooms in a dwelling predicted energy consumption.

Another factor indicative of the greater financial burden of the elderly in meeting energy costs has been cutbacks of necessities essential for daily subsistence. The United States Senate Committee on Aging (1982) related numerous instances of elderly cutting purchases of necessities in response to energy costs. Cooper (1981) supported this finding, but Royce and Iams (1982) concluded that elderly were managing better than expected and appeared to be meeting basic needs quite adequately.

Education also appeared to have an impact on energy conservation beliefs and behaviors of various age groups and income levels. Cunningham and Lopreato (1977) found less educated and low income people used the least amount of energy. Morrison et al., (1978) found that well educated, higher income families used the most energy. Contrastingly, Junk, Junk and Jones (1987) found as education increased the amount of energy consumed decreased. This reflects the findings that higher income, well educated persons are more concerned with the energy problem (Gilly & Gleb, 1978; Morrison et al., 1978).

A unique set of circumstances mitigated by income and life cycle stage appear to influence energy consumption of the elderly population. However, the studies thus far appear to be contradictory. A number of researchers have concluded that the energy consumed by the elderly is nondiscretionary because of life cycle factors and income, therefore allowing little potential for change (Cunningham & Lopreato, 1977; Newman & Day, 1975). However, Brown and Rollinson (1985) refuted that conclusion indicating that part of elderly residential energy consumption does have a discretionary component thereby suggesting that public efforts to promote energy conservation may nave missed an important population.

The purpose of this study was to investigate the residential energy beliefs and behaviors of urban elderly by income levels. More specifically, how have changes in the cost of energy impacted elderly lifestyles and to what extent do elderly favor or oppose future energy policies?

METHODOLOGY

Data

The data for this study were taken from a longitudinal survey conducted by the Western Regional Agricultural Experiment Station Committee (W-159), "Consequences of Energy Conservation Policies for Western Region Households" (Anderson et al., 1987). Ten western states (Arizona, California, Colorado, Idaho, Montana, Nevada, Oregon, Utah, Washington, and Wyoming) and Pennsylvania participated in the 1981 study. In 1983, all of the original states except Montana and California participated in the project. For this study, only data collected in 1983 from the eight western states were used.

Samples were chosen for each state and then combined for a regional sample. The 1983 sample consisted of two groups. One group was the respondents from the 1981 sample. The second group was a new sample. Both the original 1981 sample and the new 1983 sample were stratified random samples of rural (not residing in a Standard Metropolitan Statistical Area) and urban (residing in a SMSA) residents. Unweighted data were used to compute descriptive statistics on the demographic and dependent variables. Weighted data were used to compute F-tests. The data were weighted to be representative of the rural/urban populations within each state and of each state's population related to the total population in the eight states. Dillman's (1978) Total Design Method for mail surveys was used for data collection because of successful questionnaire return rates in other research using the method.

In 1983, 7,306 usable questionnaires were returned in the western states for a completion rate of 62.4 percent. The analyses in this study were completed using the urban, elderly (65-98 years of age) respondents who had indicated their income categories. The sample for the study was $N = 522$. The housing of the urban elderly and the rural elderly differ as do their incomes, thus making separate analyses desirable (Atchley & Miller, 1975).

Dependent Variables

Belief in the energy problem measured how serious (not serious to very serious) the respondent presumed the energy problem to be during the next 20 years. Energy curtailment behavior identified the number of energy curtailment measures the respondents performed at the time of the survey. Energy curtailment measures included closing off rooms, water heater set to 120°F or less, setting thermostat at 65°F or lower in winter and 78°F or higher in summer, changing the use of rooms to take advantage of sun-warmed or shaded areas, and opening and closing window coverings. Lifestyle cutbacks measured the extent (none, better, some, a lot) to which energy costs had caused changes in lifestyle. Lifestyle cutback items included groceries, meals out, driving the car, health care, vacations, recreation, education, housing, purchase of appliances or furnishings, savings and clothing. Attitudes toward future energy policy directions measured the extent to which respondents favored or opposed (strongly oppose to strongly favor) six energy policies. The six energy policies included a requirement for thermostats to be no higher than 65°F in winter and no lower than 78°F in summer, require home energy audits, require utility charges to be lowest for low energy users and highest for high users, provide larger tax credits for improved home energy efficiency, and encourage state rather than federal energy conservation programs.

Independent Variable

Income was a categorical variable describing total family income before taxes. Nine levels ranged from less than $5,000 to $50,000 or more. For the purpose of this study the nine levels were combined into four categories (less than $10,000; $10,000-$14,999; $15,000-$24,999; $25,000 or more). These four categories were based on the U.S. Bureau of the Census (1985) mean income ($15,869) of individuals 65 years and older from all race categories. The income categories were defined rather narrowly for this study and do not directly measure total available resources or net worth.

Control Variables

Household size was measured by the total number of persons who lived in the household. Education of respondent identified the level of education ranging from "0-8 grade education" to a graduate degree. Tenure of dwelling identified renters and owners. The physical size of the dwelling was determined by the respondent's estimate of square footage of the dwelling measured in increments of 500 square feet. Age of house and number of years in residency were also included as control variables. Respondents perception of the energy efficiency of the home was measured by a categorical variable ranging from "as energy efficient as possible" to "a lot of improvement to be made."

Hypotheses and Statistical Analyses

H_o1: Urban elderly by income levels do not differ in their belief in the energy problem mean scores when controlled for possible correlated variables.

H_o2: Urban elderly by income levels do not differ in their energy curtailment behavior mean scores when controlled for possible correlated variables.

H_o3: Urban elderly by income levels do not differ in their energy lifestyle cutback mean scores when controlled for possible correlated variables.

H_o4: Urban elderly by income levels do not differ in their future energy direction mean scores when controlled by possible correlated variables.

Scoring procedures for dependent variables. Respondents' belief in the energy problem scores were measured as coded: one through four with one indicating "not a serious problem" to four indicating "a very serious problem." Energy curtailment behavior mean scores were computed for respondents and were derived by dividing the number of curtailment behaviors currently performed by six, the total number identified on the questionnaire. To be given lifestyle cutback mean scores, respondents had to have answered seven or more of the II cutback items. Mean scores were calculated based on the number (7-11) answered. Similarly, future energy policy mean scores were calculated for respondents who had replied to at least four of the six policy options.

Hypotheses Testing

Kendall correlation coefficients between control variables and dependent variables were completed to determine the strengths of relationships between variables. Control variables that were not correlated at the .05 level of significance with a dependent variable were dropped out in the analysis of covariance of that dependent variable. Multiple Classification Analysis was completed to determine mean scores.

FINDINGS

Sample Description

Frequency distributions were completed on unweighted data in order to describe the respondents by socio-demographic characteristics. The urban, elderly respondents ($N = 522$) included any urban respondents from the 1983 western regional sample who answered 65 years or older and indicated income categories. The mean age of the urban elderly respondents was 71.6 years with 32.8 percent being female and 65.3 percent male. Income distributions ranged from 25.7 percent having less than $10,000, 18.8 percent in $10,000-$14,999; 27.4 percent in $15,000-$24,999; and 28.2 percent in $25,000 or more. The median income was in the $15,000-$24,999 category. The median education level was completion of trade school after high school graduation. Approximately 66 percent of the respondents were married at the time of the survey with 5.0 percent having experienced divorce, 25.9 percent widowed, and 3.1 percent separated or never married. The majority of respondents (83.9 percent) owned their homes (with 5.2 percent of the owned dwellings located in condominium complexes) and 11.3 percent rented. The majority of elderly respondents (66.5 percent) resided in single family detached houses. The median year the dwellings were built was 1960.

Analyses and Discussion

The control variables which were correlated with each dependent variable (Table 1) were included in each analysis of covariance test. Four analyses of covariance using weighted data were used to test hypothesized relationships.

Belief in the energy problem. To determine the degree to which urban elderly believe in the energy problem, respondents were asked whether or not they thought that the energy problem would be serious over the next 20 years. An analysis of covariance test was completed to determine whether belief in the energy problem was

Table 1. Kendall Correlation Coefficients

Dependent Variables	Control Variables						
	Household Size	Education	Tenure	Physical Size of Dwelling	Age of Dwelling	Years of Residency	Energy Efficiency
Belief in energy problem	-.0342	.0827*	-.0164	.0737*	.0450	.0549	.0577
Curtailment behaviors	-.0540	-.0220	.0741*	.0131	.0402	.0667*	.0031
Lifestyle cutbacks	-.0789*	-.1667*	-.0811*	-.1994*	-.0251	.0354	.0416
Future energy policy directions	-.0524	-.1050*	.0019	-.0422	.0557*	.0384	.0208

* = p ≤ .05

influenced by income when controlled for education or size of the dwelling (Table 2). The results show no significant difference between belief in the problem and income (p = .869), or either covariate: education (p = .083) or size of dwelling (p = .427).

The results of this analysis reveal that income when controlled for education and size of dwelling does not influence belief in the energy problem among urban elderly, although previous research had found age, income, and education to be significant determinants of belief in the energy problem. Johnson-Carroll (1986) found belief in the energy problem was significantly (*p* < .05) related to education and age. Younger respondents and those with higher levels of education were more likely to believe in the seriousness of the energy problem. Gilly and Gleb (1978) and Katz and Morgan (1983) not only concurred but also found that respondents who earned higher incomes were more likely to believe in the seriousness of the problem. Although size of dwelling had been found to be a good predictor of money spent on home energy (Marganus, 1984; Morrison et al., 1978; Tyler, Lovingood, Bowen & Tyler, 1982), Johnson-Carroll (1986) found belief in the energy problem not related to dwelling size, a finding further supported by this study.

Previous researchers who compared age inclusive samples had found that the elderly as a group believed less in the energy problem. By including income, which had been found to be a significant belief determinant in age inclusive research, it was felt that some variation in belief in the energy problem among the urban elderly might be found. However, income when controlled for education and size of dwelling was not found to be a predictor of differences in belief in the energy problem among the urban elderly.

Energy curtailment behavior. To explore for differences among urban elderly respondents, no cost energy curtailment measures, energy curtailment behavior mean scores were tested by analysis of covariance (Table 2). Income (p = .044) when controlled for tenure (p = .017) was found to be significantly related to curtailment behavior, while the covariate years of residency (p = 901) was not. The adjusted mean scores from the Multiple Classification Analysis indicated an inverse relationship whereby an increase in income level was related to a decrease in curtailment behaviors.

Researchers had shown that older people engaged in energy curtailment behavior less often than younger people (Eichner & Morris, 1984; Johnson-Carroll, 1986). Some felt that older respondents often used energy to maintain well-being and were reluctant to engage in conservation practices if those practices affected health (Eichner & Morris, 1984; Royce & Iams, 1982). Eichner and Morris (1984) also found elderly to be less open to making energy-conserving changes to their homes. Even so, in this study elderly respondents were involved in a mean of three of the six energy curtailment practices identified. Although the numerical difference in mean scores among the elderly income categories was small, the urban elderly with lower incomes engaged in more energy curtailment behaviors than respondents with higher incomes. Previous research has found that lower income individuals do not complete structural modifications. Consequently, those in this income category may be more inclined to use low cost energy curtailment measures to reduce energy costs (Eichner & Morris, 1984; Katz & Morgan, 1983). Similar findings hold true regarding tenure of the dwelling. Homeowners are more likely to live in energy efficient dwellings thus reducing the need to engage in a large number of conservation measures (Johnson-Carroll, 1986). Eighty-three percent of the respondents in this study own their own homes. Although the largest number of respondents owning their own homes would probably fall in the upper income category, this issue was not addressed in this study.

Lifestyle cutbacks. In order to determine whether there were differences among the elderly in lifestyle cutbacks, respondents were asked to identify which cutbacks, if any, had occurred due to an increase in energy costs. Analysis of covariance tests revealed that income ($p = .000$) was significantly related to lifestyle cutbacks, when controlled for education ($p = .000$) and size of dwelling ($p = .000$) (Table 2). Two covariates, household size ($p = .604$) and tenure ($p = .718$), were not significantly related to cutbacks. The adjusted mean scores indicate an inverse relationship, as income increases, lifestyle cutbacks decrease.

The results of this research indicate that elderly are experiencing different lifestyle cutbacks among income levels which has also been reported by Cooper (1981) and the United States Senate Com-

Table 2.

Dependent Variable:	aBelief in Energy Problem	bEnergy Curtailment Behavior	cLifestyle Cutbacks	dFuture Energy Policy Directions
n (weighted data)5:	614	650	665	664
Independent Variable:	Income	Income*	Income*	Income
Control Variable:	Education	Years of Residency	Education*	Age of Dwelling*
	Size of Dwelling	Tenure*	Household Size	Education*
			Size of Dwelling*	
			Tenure	

Adjusted Mean Scores

Income Levels ($)				
1. <10,000	2.89	3.47	2.53	3.23
2. 10,000-14,999	2.95	3.38	2.18	3.33
3. 15,000-24,999	2.98	3.25	1.81	3.22
4. 25,000+	2.96	3.15	1.68	3.21

1) Response Scales Dependent Variables: a_1 - Not Serious through 4 - Very Serious

   b_6 - Energy Saving Practices

   c_1 - None through 4 - A Lot

   d_1 - Strongly Oppose through 5 - Strongly Favor

2) Mean scores were adjusted for significant independent and control variables for each dependent variable and income level.

3) Lifestyle Cutbacks: Respondents answered 7 out of 12 lifestyle cutbacks.

4) The statistical test performed on weighted data was an F-test.

   * $p < .05$

   ** $p < .01$

   *** $p < .001$

5) n varies due to missing cases; n is representative of the weighted urban sample.

mittee on Aging (1982). Lower income elderly experience more lifestyle cutbacks than higher income elderly. A higher income often coincides with a larger dwelling and more actual dollars spent on energy costs (Marganus, 1984; Newman & Day, 1975), while a lower income results in a smaller dwelling which uses less energy but may require proportionally more dollars to pay for energy costs (Katz & Morgan, 1983; Newman & Day, 1975). Thus, it seems that a larger proportion of income spent on increasing energy costs would require cutbacks on other necessities.

Future energy policy directions. To determine receptivity to future energy policy directions, respondents were asked to identify the degree of opposition or favorability toward future energy policies. Analysis of covariance revealed that income ($p = .277$) was not significantly related to future energy policy directions (Table 2). Two covariates, age of dwelling ($p = .03$) and education ($p = .003$), were significantly related to future energy policy directions. The adjusted mean scores revealed that respondents, regardless of income level, were neutral toward future energy policy directions. Merfeld (1984) found that significant socio demographic characteristics varied depending on the regulations being investigated. Personal impact or inconvenience determined respondents attitudes toward specific regulations or directions. In this study, a future energy direction mean score was calculated for each respondent. This could explain the neutrality of results. Based on Merfeld's findings, respondents could favor certain policy directions and oppose others. Therefore, it could be more meaningful to investigate attitudes toward individual policies.

IMPLICATIONS

Although public attention toward residential energy costs has diminished, belief in the seriousness of the energy problem remains a concern for the elderly. The results of this research indicate that urban elderly with lower incomes engage in more lifestyle cutbacks and curtailment behaviors than those with higher incomes. The results emphasize the fact that low income urban elderly may be adversely affected by energy costs. Policies and programs should address the needs of this unique population. Although no conclusion was reached in this study regarding future policy directions, further research needs to investigate not only the establishment of relevant energy policies but also whether the low income elderly would be receptive to those potential policies.

Additionally, further research is needed which focuses on low income elderly from rural and urban settings in various geographic locations. What impact do energy costs have on lifestyle cutbacks and curtailment behaviors of elderly in each of these settings? How might this information impact policies and programs in specific locations?

The cost of energy will continue to be a perennial problem for low income elderly. It is important to continue investigation of this area so basic needs of the elderly population are adequately met.

REFERENCES

Anderson, M. A., Iams, D., Jones, J. C., Chatelain, L. B., Dillman, D. A., & Anderson, D. A. (1987). *Energy directions for the Western United States: A western perspective, 1981-1983.*

Atchley, R. C., & Miller, S. J. (1975). Housing and the rural aged. *Rural Environments and Aging.*

Brown, M. A., & Rollinson, P. A. (1985). Residential energy consumption in low-income and elderly households: How nondiscretionary is it? *Energy Systems and Policy, 9,* 271-301.

Coltrane, S., Archer, D., & Aronson, E. (1986). The social-psychological foundations of successful energy conservation programmes. *Energy Policy, 14*(2), 133-148.

Cook, F. L., & Kramek, L. M. (1986). Measuring economic hardship among older Americans. *Gerontologist, 26*(1), 38-47.

Cooper, S. (1981). Fuel bills and the elderly. *Aging* (Jan.-Feb.):11-17.

Cunningham, W. H., & Lopreato, S. (1977). *Energy use and conservation incentives: A study of the southwestern United States.* New York: Praeger Publishers.

Dillman, D. A. (1978). *Mail and telephone survey: The total design method.* New York: John Wiley and Sons.

Eichner, M. M., & Morris, E. M. (1984). Energy conservation, air quality, health, and housing satisfaction. *Housing and Society, 11*(1), 1-15.

Gibbons, J. H., & Chandler, W. U. (1981). *Energy: The conservation revolution.* New York: The Plenum Press.

Gilly, M. C., & Gelb, B. D. (1978, Winter). Marketing energy conservation. *Journal of Home Economics, 70,* 31-33.

Hirst, E. (1985). Is improved energy efficiency still an important policy issue? *Energy Policy, 13*(2), 115-116.

Johnson-Carroll, K. J. A. (1986). *Factors that influence energy conservation alterations in Oregon households.* Unpublished doctoral dissertation, Oregon State University, Corvallis, OR.

Junk, V., Junk, W. S., & Jones, J. C. (1987). Impact of energy audits on home energy consumption. *Journal of Consumer Studies and Home Economics 11,* 21-38.

Katz, E., & Morgan, S. (1983, October 9-11). *The financing of energy conservation services to low income households: Alternatives to grants.* Paper presented at the Energy Crisis and Families Conference, Michigan State University, East Lansing, MI.

Kennedy, J. M. (1980). Residential energy costs and their impact on housing costs of elderly and low income. *Proceedings of the 1980 annual meeting of the American Association of Housing Educators Conference*: 77-85.

Longman, P. (1985). Supporting retirees: Justice between generations. *Current, 275,* 8-16.

Marganus, M. (1984). *A market oriented approach to energy conservation: Identifying disadvantaged families as target groups for energy assistance programs.* Unpublished doctoral dissertation, Oregon State University, Corvallis, OR.

Marganus, M., & Badenhop, S. (1984). Energy expenditures and family well being by stages in the family life-cycle. *Conference proceedings: Families and energy: coping with uncertainty* (pp. 391-404). East Lansing Michigan: Michigan State University Press.

Merfeld, M. K. (1984). *Consumer attitudes toward potentially restrictive energy conservation regulations.* Unpublished doctoral dissertation, Oregon State University, Corvallis, OR.

Morrison, B. M., & Gladhart, P. M. (1976). Energy and families: The crisis and the response. *Journal of Home Economics 68* (1):15-18.

Morrison, B. M., Gladhart, P. M., Zuiches, J. J., Keith, J. G., Keefe, D., & Long, B. R. (1978, Winter). Energy and families: The crisis and the response. *Journal of Home Economics, 70,* 19-21.

Newman, D. K., & Day, D. (1975). *The American energy consumer.* Massachusetts: Ballinger Publishing.

Pepmiller, E. G. (1981). Conserve heat and live. *Aging* (Jan-Feb):16-17.

Pitts, J. M. (1986). Planning for tomorrows elderly. *Family Economics Review, 2*(4), 17-20.

Royce, V., & Iams, D. (1982). Coping with rising energy costs: A look at the older people in Arizona. *Proceedings of the 22nd Annual Home Management-Family Economics Educators Conference* (pp. 106-110).

Savitz, M. L. (1984). Ten years out — a problem not a crisis. *Conference proceedings; Families and energy: Coping with uncertainty* (pp. 7-9). East Lansing, Michigan: Michigan State University Press.

Tyler, L. L., Lovingood, R. P., Bowen, S. P., & Tyler, R. F. (1982). Energy related characteristics of low income tenants. *Housing and Society, 9*(3), 9-15.

U.S. Senate Committee on Aging. (1982). *Energy and the aged: The widening gap.* Washington, D.C.: U.S. Government Printing Office.

U.S. Bureau of the Census. (1985). *Statistical abstract of the United States.* 105 Edition, Income, Expenditures, and Wealth. Washington, DC: U.S. Government Printing Office.

Warriner, G. D. (1981). Electricity consumption by the elderly: Policy implications. *The Journal of Consumer Research, 8*:258-264.

White, B. J. (1985). *Housing America's elderly population.* Unpublished manuscript, College of Home Economics, Oregon State University, Corvallis.

Chapter 9

Continuing/Life Care Facilities and the Continuum of Care

Diane E. Alperin
Nicholas D. Richie

SUMMARY. The proliferation of continuing/life care facilities in the United States in recent years holds the promise of providing retirees with a full continuum of care. This survey of continuing/life care facilities in the state of Florida was undertaken to ascertain if they indeed were providing the services necessary to fulfill this promise. The results indicate that only a small percentage of continuing/life care facilities offer all the services the authors believe necessary for a full continuum of care, with shelter care being the least frequently offered service.

INTRODUCTION

The proliferation of continuing/life care (hereafter C/LC) facilities in the United States in recent years holds the promise of providing retirees with a full continuum of care—ranging from independent living in separate residential units to skilled nursing care (Raper, 1984). When one considers that many of these facilities require substantial up-front endowments or entrance fees, which may or may not be returned in whole or in part (Raper, 1984), it becomes evident that a need exists to explore the extent to which the

Diane E. Alperin, MS, is affiliated with the Social Work Program.
Nicholas D. Richie, MSW, PhD, is affiliated with the Health Administration Program, Florida Atlantic University, 500 NW 20th Street, ADM, Boca Raton, FL 33431.

125

promise of this continuum of care is being met in reality. It was with this purpose in mind that the authors of this report recently surveyed C/LC facilities in Florida — a state which contains both a disproportionate percentage of population (17.3%) over age 65 (U.S. Department of Commerce, 1981), and about 10% of C/LC facilities which have been identified nationwide (Department of Insurance and Treasurer, 1984) — again representing a disproportionate share when compared with other states (Raper, 1984).

PROCEDURE

The Department of Insurance and Treasurer of the State of Florida supplied a list of 68 facilities, in June 1984, identified as providing C/LC (Department of Insurance and Treasurer, 1984). Of these, 2 proved to be duplicate listings, and another had recently converted to a general rental complex — leaving a population of 66. An anonymous questionnaire was sent to the administrators of these facilities requesting, among other data, information on the services available at the facility. Twenty-three (35%) of the questionnaires were returned and analyzed for this report.

The authors defined the continuum of care in its fullest sense to range from independent living on one end, to skilled nursing care on the other. Eight specific services were assumed to be necessary in order to claim such a continuum of care was available:

1. The provision of at least one prepared meal, per day, for those who chose not to cook, or desired the social benefits of a communal meal, or needed professional dietary supervision at least part of the day to compensate for any nutritional shortcomings in the meals which were self-prepared in the independent living units.
2. An emergency call service available from the individual living units.
3. Assistance-in-living in the apartment, when needed, such as housekeeping services, personal care services, etc.
4. Home health services available in the individual living units.
5. A sheltered care unit available outside the residential apart-

ments, assignment to which is based on an assessment of a need for less-than-nursinghome care.
6. Social work counseling available to all residents in the apartments.
7. A skilled nursing care facility on the grounds.
8. Additional social work counseling available to patients in the skilled nursing facility.

Thus, the authors created an "ideal" comprehensive continuum of care, consisting of 8 services, against which the institutions surveyed could be measured. This report summarizes the extent to which the facilities studied met this ideal.

FINDINGS

Table 1 contains a frequency distribution showing the number of facilities offering from 1-8 elements from the "ideal" continuum of care. As can be seen, only one facility offered all 8 services, but 65% (15) offered at least 6 of the services.

Table 2 contains the frequency, in descending order, with which

TABLE 1

Frequency Distribution of the Number of Continuum of Care Services Offered in Twenty-Three Continuing/Life Care Facilities

Number of Facilities (N=23)	Number of Continuum of Care Services Offered
1	8
6	7
8	6
1	5
3	4
2	3
2	2
0	1

TABLE 2

The Frequency of Continuum of Care Services Offered in Twenty-Three
Continuing/Life Care Facilities (In Descending Order of Frequency)

Continuum of Care Service	Frequency Mentioned
Emergency call service	22 (95.65%)
Skilled nursing home	19 (82.6%)
At least one meal daily	18 (78.2%)
Assistance-in-living	17 (73.91%)
Social service for apartment residents	14 (60.8%)
Social service in the nursing home	14 (60.8%)
Home health care	12 (52.17%)
Shelter care	9 (39.13%)

each of the 8 services was found at the institutions in the sample. As
can be seen, all but one facility (95.65%) offered emergency call
services. At the other extreme, only 9 (39.13%) of these facilities
offered shelter care.

DISCUSSION

To the extent that these findings are generalizable to the state of
Florida in particular and to C/LC facilities nationwide, one would
expect only a small percentage of such facilities to offer all 8 services identified by these authors as representing a reasonable inter-
pretation of the full continuum of care likely to be expected by
prospective residents. However, the majority of facilities are likely
to offer 6 or more of these services. When one looks at the specific
services offered, only shelter care is shown in Table 2 to be offered
by less than 50% of the institutions surveyed—suggesting that perhaps residents in need of such care may instead be receiving assistance-in-living in their apartments or skilled nursing care in the
complex's nursing home facility. When coupled with the 52% of
facilities offering home health care, the impression that the contin-

uum of care from independent living to skilled nursing care may in reality be less complete than expected, is additionally reinforced. The three most-frequently mentioned services — emergency call service, skilled nursing care, and at least one meal daily, may represent a nucleus of services which largely defines the distinguishing characteristics of continuing/life care as they exist in reality, rather then ideally.

CONCLUSION

This sample of C/LC facilities in Florida calls into question, to the degree that it is generalizable, the extent to which one can assume such facilities actually offer a complete continuum of care from independent apartment living to skilled nursing care, for those who opt for such an arrangement. The 8-point continuum proposed by the researchers was only fulfilled by one institution, although 65% of the facilities offered at least 6 of these services. Service seemed to be most infrequent where needed to provide a half-way sheltered facility for residents to avoid nursing home placement — when staying in one's independent residential unit is temporarily not recommended. In addition, the availability of home health care services in the residential unit was also identified by only slightly more than half the sample — again calling into question the extent to which such facilities can provide services at discrete points on the proposed continuum of care, rather than mainly at the two extreme locations — the resident's apartment or the skilled nursing home.

General inflation in the economy is contributing to increases both in the entrance fees/endowments necessary in C/LC and the monthly fee schedules (Raper, 1984) — and the extent to which the expected services for continuity of care are truly available to consumers is therefore a crucial research question. Beyond that, related questions may include an evaluation of each of the identified services, for example. Perhaps some are not actually much in demand, and therefore from a cost-benefit standpoint are not absolutely necessary, and can be foregone without jeopardizing the *overall* quality of the experience for those elderly who opt for such a living arrangement. Perhaps the absence of others, such as shelter care, leads to unmet need or the inappropriate use of other services, such as the skilled nursing care facility. These and related questions are fertile areas for future research in this burgeoning sector of retirement living.

REFERENCES

Department of Insurance and Treasurer, Bureau of Allied Lines, The Capitol, Tallahassee, Florida 32301, Communication, June 1984.

Raper, Ann Trueblood. *National Continuing Care Directory*. Glenview, Illinois: Scott, Foresman and Company, 1984.

United States Department of Commerce, Bureau of the Census. *Population Profile of the United States 1981* Washington D.C.: Government Printing Office, 1982, Table 3-4.